1

This book belongs to:

_____

Capricorn Daily Horoscope 2025

Author's Note: Time set to Coordinated Universal Time Zone (UT±0)

Contents

The 12 Zodiac Star Signs

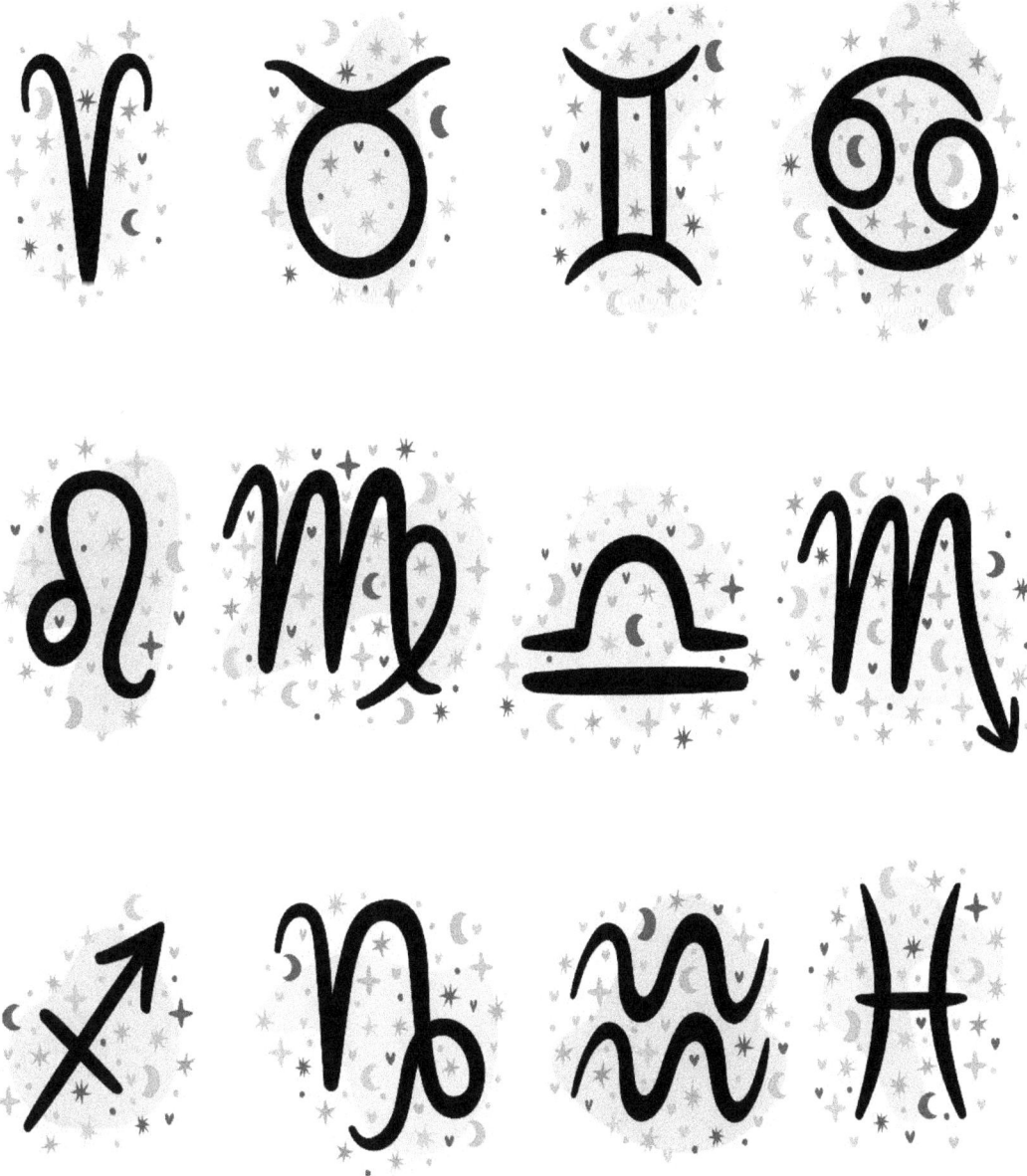

2025

January

S	M	T	W	T	F	S
			1	2	3	4
5	6	7	8	9	10	11
12	13	14	15	16	17	18
19	20	21	22	23	24	25
26	27	28	29	30	31	

February

S	M	T	W	T	F	S
						1
2	3	4	5	6	7	8
9	10	11	12	13	14	15
16	17	18	19	20	21	22
23	24	25	26	27	28	

March

S	M	T	W	T	F	S
						1
2	3	4	5	6	7	8
9	10	11	12	13	14	15
16	17	18	19	20	21	22
23	24	25	26	27	28	29
30	31					

April

S	M	T	W	T	F	S
		1	2	3	4	5
6	7	8	9	10	11	12
13	14	15	16	17	18	19
20	21	22	23	24	25	26
27	28	29	30			

May

S	M	T	W	T	F	S
				1	2	3
4	5	6	7	8	9	10
11	12	13	14	15	16	17
18	19	20	21	22	23	24
25	26	27	28	29	30	31

June

S	M	T	W	T	F	S
1	2	3	4	5	6	7
8	9	10	11	12	13	14
15	16	17	18	19	20	21
22	23	24	25	26	27	28
29	30					

July

S	M	T	W	T	F	S
		1	2	3	4	5
6	7	8	9	10	11	12
13	14	15	16	17	18	19
20	21	22	23	24	25	26
27	28	29	30	31		

August

S	M	T	W	T	F	S
					1	2
3	4	5	6	7	8	9
10	11	12	13	14	15	16
17	18	19	20	21	22	23
24	25	26	27	28	29	30
31						

September

S	M	T	W	T	F	S
	1	2	3	4	5	6
7	8	9	10	11	12	13
14	15	16	17	18	19	20
21	22	23	24	25	26	27
28	29	30				

October

S	M	T	W	T	F	S
			1	2	3	4
5	6	7	8	9	10	11
12	13	14	15	16	17	18
19	20	21	22	23	24	25
26	27	28	29	30	31	

November

S	M	T	W	T	F	S
						1
2	3	4	5	6	7	8
9	10	11	12	13	14	15
16	17	18	19	20	21	22
23	24	25	26	27	28	29
30						

December

S	M	T	W	T	F	S
	1	2	3	4	5	6
7	8	9	10	11	12	13
14	15	16	17	18	19	20
21	22	23	24	25	26	27
28	29	30	31			

2025

Daily Horoscope

CAPRICORN

As your astrologer, I wish to explain why one horoscope book may differ from another for each zodiac sign. The vast array of astrological activity constantly occurring in the sky requires me to focus on the essential aspect of the star sign I am writing for on any given day. Each zodiac sign is unique, and the various planetary factors affect them differently.

When crafting horoscopes, I pay special attention to the significant astrological aspects directly impacting a specific sign. By doing so, I can provide the most insightful and relevant guidance to individuals of that zodiac sign. While there might be multiple planetary alignments on a particular day, one aspect may hold more significance for a specific sign than others.

Considering the ruling planets and elements associated with each zodiac sign further refines my interpretations. This attention to detail ensures that the horoscope resonates with the distinct characteristics and tendencies of the star sign in question.

Ultimately, I aim to offer personalized insights and advice based on each zodiac sign's unique cosmic influences. By focusing on each star sign's most relevant astrological aspects, I can help readers better understand themselves and navigate the energies surrounding them. Embracing each zodiac sign's strengths, challenges, and opportunities allows me to create a horoscope book tailored to my readers' needs.

"We are born at a given moment, in a given place, and, like vintage years of wine, we have the qualities of the year and the season of which we are born. Astrology does not lay claim to anything more."

—Carl Jung

JANUARY

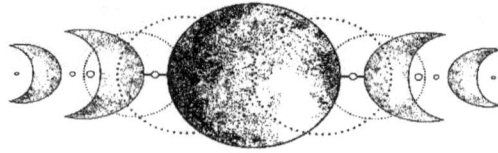

MOON MAGIC

Sun	Mon	Tue	Wed	Thu	Fri	Sat
			1	2	3	4
5	6	7	8	9	10	11
12	13	14	15	16	17	18
19	20	21	22	23	24	25
26	27	28	29	30	31	

New Moon

WOLF MOON

30 Monday

With the Moon ingress Capricorn and the arrival of the New Moon, you may feel a sense of determination and focus in achieving your goals. Your practicality and discipline come to the forefront, allowing you to progress steadily and take calculated steps toward success. It's a time to establish a structured plan and take charge of your future. Embrace the energy of this New Moon to plant seeds of intention and build a stable framework for your aspirations.

31 Tuesday

New Year's Eve offers celebration and revelry, with parties and fireworks lighting the night sky. You enjoy delicious food and drinks, dance to upbeat music, and connect with others in a festive atmosphere. It's a time to let loose and have fun, celebrating all you have accomplished and looking forward to what's to come. New Year's Eve is a time of reflection, renewal, and celebration. It's a chance to leave behind the old and embrace the new with hope and optimism for the future.

1 Wednesday

This New Year's Day, as the Moon enters Aquarius, you may feel a surge of excitement and a desire for change and innovation. This lunar influence encourages you to embrace uniqueness and think outside the box. It's a time to break free from old patterns and embrace new perspectives. You may find yourself drawn to social causes and groups. Use this energy to set intentions and goals that align with your authentic self and contribute positively to the collective.

2 Thursday

As you navigate your daily routine, the cosmic orchestration prompts a recalibration of your habits and rituals. Embrace the call for positive change and incorporate mindful practices into your day-to-day life. The celestial energies encourage you to find a harmonious balance between productivity and self-care, fostering a daily rhythm that nourishes your body, mind, and spirit. Seize the opportunity to create a routine that aligns with your overall well-being.

3 Friday

As Venus enters Pisces, you may feel a heightened sense of compassion and emotional depth in your relationships. As the Moon enters Pisces, it adds emotional and dreamy energy. This celestial alignment is a time to honor emotions, embrace imagination, and find solace in creative and spiritual pursuits. Allow yourself to dive deep into your inner world and connect with the universal energy flow. Trust your intuition and use this time to heal and find inner peace.

4 Saturday

The Sun forms a sextile aspect with Saturn, which signifies a time of stability, discipline, and accomplishment. This alignment encourages you to take a responsible and structured approach to your goals and ambitions. This harmonious connection between the Sun and Saturn empowers you to take on challenges with patience, determination, and a strategic mindset. It's favorable for planning, organizing, and taking practical steps toward your aspirations.

5 Sunday

The Aries Moon empowers you to assert your individuality and express your authentic self. It's a time to trust your instincts and follow your passions wholeheartedly. You might desire independence, pushing you to take the lead and initiate new projects. Embrace this dynamic energy, channel it into productive outlets, and fearlessly go after what you want. The Moon in Aries reminds you to be true to yourself and fearlessly embrace the adventures that await you.

6 Monday

With Mercury Square Neptune, there may be a challenge in clear communication and decision-making. Your thoughts and perceptions may be clouded by confusion or illusion, making it essential to stay grounded and seek clarity before making meaningful choices. It's crucial to be cautious of deception or misunderstandings in your interactions. Take the time to reflect, gather accurate information, and trust your intuition to navigate any potential confusion.

7 Tuesday

With the Moon entering Taurus, you may experience a sense of stability and groundedness in your emotions. Embrace the energy of the Moon in Taurus by cultivating patience, practicality, and a deep appreciation for the simple pleasures in life. Engage in activities that connect with nature, indulge in delicious meals, and create a harmonious environment that supports your well-being. Trust your instincts and allow yourself to savor the moment, finding beauty and tranquility.

8 Wednesday

With Mercury entering Capricorn, you may notice a shift in your thinking and communication style. Your mind becomes more focused, practical, and structured. This influence encourages you to think strategically and organize, making it a good time for planning, setting goals, and working towards long-term objectives. You will likely approach conversations and decision-making thoughtfully and deliberately, valuing logic and practicality.

9 Thursday

In the first house, your Capricorn Sun radiates a strong sense of discipline and ambition, shaping your personality with a focus on responsibility and achievement. You approach life with a pragmatic and strategic mindset, often setting long-term goals and working diligently to attain them. Your public image is marked by competence and reliability, and you may be drawn to leadership roles where your organizational skills can shine.

10 Friday

With the Moon ingress Gemini, your emotional state can fluctuate, as the Moon in Gemini brings a mix of lightheartedness and restlessness. It is a good time for learning, gathering knowledge, and engaging in intellectual pursuits. Your curiosity heightens, and you may easily engage in discussions and debates. Embrace this energy by engaging in activities stimulating your mind, connecting with others through communication, and exploring new ideas.

11 Saturday

In the realm of home life, the cosmic energies usher in a period of domestic harmony and familial bonds. Embrace the opportunity to strengthen connections with loved ones, fostering a supportive and nurturing environment. Whether through shared meals, heart-to-heart conversations, or collaborative activities, the celestial forces encourage you to cultivate a home that serves as both a refuge and a source of inspiration.

12 Sunday

With the Moon entering Cancer and Mars forming a trine with Neptune, you are in for heightened emotional sensitivity and creative inspiration. The Moon in Cancer nurtures your emotional well-being, emphasizing the need for comfort, security, and connection with loved ones. As your intuition and emotional depth heighten, you may seek solace in familiar surroundings and unique relationships. It is a time to honor feelings and find comfort in home and family.

13 Monday

With the Sun forming a trine with Uranus and a Full Moon illuminating the sky, you are in for exciting breakthroughs and heightened awareness. The Sun trine Uranus aspect brings your life a sense of liberation and innovation. It encourages you to embrace your unique individuality and express yourself authentically. You may feel a surge of inspiration and a desire for change as you seek new experiences and perspectives.

14 Tuesday

The Moon's ingress into Leo amplifies your passion, creativity, and desire for recognition. You may feel a strong urge to shine your light and express yourself authentically in various areas of your life. This alignment encourages you to embrace individuality, confidently share your talents, and seek joy and pleasure in your experiences. However, the square between Venus and Jupiter requires balance and moderation.

15 Wednesday

In the destined tapestry of your career, the celestial energies whisper of a transformative moment on the horizon. You stand on the cusp of change, a cosmic dance that promises growth and evolution. This auspicious phase invites you to spread your wings and explore new pathways in your professional journey. As the celestial currents guide you, embrace the optimism that accompanies this shift, propelling you toward unprecedented heights in your career.

16 Thursday

The Sun-opposed Mars aspect can bring about a strong urge for action and assertion but can also lead to impatience and conflicts. You may feel a heightened sense of drive and ambition, but tempering this energy with patience and careful consideration is essential. The Moon's ingress into Virgo adds a touch of practicality and attention to detail to the mix. It encourages you to analyze and organize your thoughts and actions.

17 Friday

With the Sun sextile Neptune, you will likely experience a harmonious blend of imagination and intuition. This aspect brings a sense of inspiration and spiritual connection into your life. You may find that your creative abilities are enhanced, allowing you to tap easily into your artistic and imaginative side. Your intuition may also be heightened during this time, guiding you toward a deeper understanding of yourself and the world around you.

18 Saturday

With Mars in Cancer gracing your seventh house, your approach to partnerships and relationships is marked by emotional intensity and a protective instinct. You invest passion and energy into creating a harmonious and secure connection with your significant others. Strive to find a balance between assertiveness and receptivity, allowing space for both independence and partnership within your relationships.

19 Sunday

Mercury's sextile to Saturn and Venus enhances your ability to communicate and express yourself clearly and sincerely. This aspect supports practical thinking, disciplined communication, and cooperative exchange of ideas. The sextile between Mercury and Venus adds a touch of charm and diplomacy to your conversations and interactions, fostering a pleasant and collaborative atmosphere. It's the perfect time to enjoy companionship and promote harmony.

20 Monday

With Venus in Pisces in the third house, your communication style is infused with sensitivity, charm, and a poetic flair. You express love and appreciation through words, and a desire marks your interactions for harmony and connection. You may find joy in creative writing or artistic forms of communication. Be cautious of potential indecisiveness and the inclination to idealize relationships, and strive for clear and open communication to foster genuine connections.

21 Tuesday

With the Sun conjunct with Pluto, you may experience a powerful transformation and intensified energy. This aspect brings deep self-awareness and the opportunity for profound inner growth. You are encouraged to explore the depths of your being, uncover hidden truths, and let go of anything that no longer serves you. As the Moon ingresses Scorpio, it amplifies the intensity of your emotions and fosters a desire for emotional depth and authenticity.

22 Wednesday

With Mercury in Capricorn in the first house, your communication style and thought processes are marked by practicality, discipline, and a strategic mindset. You approach life with a logical and organized approach, valuing precision in your thoughts and words. Your mental focus is often directed towards personal goals and achievements, and you may excel in leadership roles where your strategic thinking and practical communication skills can shine.

23 Thursday

Mercury trine Uranus offers a solution by bringing a touch of brilliance and originality to your thoughts and ideas. This aspect enhances your mental agility and allows you to think outside the box, finding inventive solutions to challenges. It's a time of intellectual stimulation and breakthroughs where you can embrace unconventional perspectives and change your habitual thinking. You can take courageous action and tap into your creative and innovative thoughts.

24 Friday

Embrace wanderlust and opportunities for growth and expansion. You may seek new cultures, philosophies, or belief systems that resonate with your quest for truth and meaning. The Moon in Sagittarius encourages you to step out of your comfort zone and embrace the unknown with optimism and an open mind. It's a time of embracing freedom, diversity, and the joy of discovering new possibilities. Use this energy to express your ideas and foster meaningful connections.

25 Saturday

You may experience a harmonious blend of passion, attraction, and creative energy with Venus trine Mars. This aspect brings a sense of balance and ease to your relationships and personal desires. Your actions align with your heart's wishes, and your assertiveness infuses you with charm and grace. This transit is an excellent time to pursue romantic connections, express affection, and enjoy pleasurable experiences.

26 Sunday

With the Moon ingress Capricorn, you experience a shift in emotional energy that emphasizes practicality and ambition. Your emotions become grounded and focused on long-term goals, prompting you to approach life responsibly and determinedly. This lunar placement encourages you to prioritize structure and stability in your personal and professional life. It enables you to follow your ambitions while staying connected to your intuitive and creative side.

27 Monday

In the second house, the Aquarius Sun directs its innovative and humanitarian energy toward matters of personal values, finances, and possessions. You approach material resources with a forward-thinking mindset, valuing independence and uniqueness. Financial stability may be linked to unconventional or progressive pursuits, and you may find fulfillment in aligning your resources with causes that promote social change.

28 Tuesday

The combination of Mercury and the Moon in Aquarius enhances your ability to think outside the box and communicate your ideas effectively. You may find yourself drawn to intellectual pursuits, group discussions, or collaborative projects that aim to bring about positive change. This transit is a time to embrace your individuality, embrace diversity, and contribute to collective efforts that have the potential to make a difference.

29 Wednesday

With Mercury conjunct with Pluto, your thoughts delve into the depths of your psyche. This alignment brings intensity and a probing nature to your mental processes. You investigate hidden truths, uncover secrets, and explore the underlying motivations behind people's words and actions. Your perception allows you to see beyond surface-level conversations. This transit empowers you to delve into research, study, or any pursuit that requires depth and concentration.

30 Thursday

Embrace the transformative energy of Uranus, the intuitive nature of the Moon in Pisces, and the expansive power of the Sun trine Jupiter. This combination offers a potent blend of liberation, spiritual connection, and growth. Be open to unexpected opportunities, trust your intuition, and embrace the positive energy surrounding you. These transits are a time of personal development, expansion, and discovering new horizons.

FEBRUARY

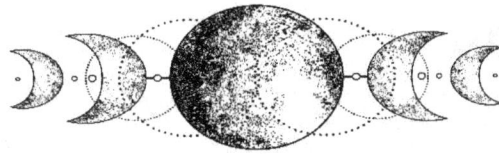

MOON MAGIC

Sun	Mon	Tue	Wed	Thu	Fri	Sat
						1
2	3	4	5	6	7	8
9	10	11	12	13	14	15
16	17	18	19	20	21	22
23	24	25	26	27	28	

NEW MOON

SNOW MOON

31 Friday

Creativity takes center stage as the celestial canvas beckons you to express your unique essence through artistic pursuits. Whether engaging in a cherished hobby, exploring new creative ventures, or collaborating with like-minded individuals, the cosmic energies invite you to unleash your imagination. Embrace the freedom to innovate and infuse your daily life with the vibrant colors of creativity, allowing this period to be a tapestry of self-expression and inspired living.

1 Saturday

With Venus conjunct with Neptune, dreamy and enchanting energy heightens your sense of beauty, romance, and spirituality. This celestial alignment invites you to explore love and relationships with magic and sensitivity. You may yearn for deep emotional connections and experience a heightened appreciation for art, music, and aesthetics. This cosmic dance between Venus and Neptune encourages your heart's desires as you embrace imagination and compassion.

2 Sunday

With the Moon entering Aries, you feel a surge of fiery energy and assertiveness within you. This lunar transit ignites your passion and encourages you to take bold action. You may find yourself driven to pursue your goals with enthusiasm and determination. It's a time to trust your instincts, embrace spontaneity, and fearlessly venture into new territory. The Aries Moon empowers you to assert your needs, set boundaries, and be true to yourself.

3 Monday

With Mercury forming a harmonious trine aspect to Jupiter, your mind expands, and your thoughts soar to new heights. This cosmic alignment brings forth a sense of optimism and intellectual growth, allowing you to see the bigger picture and embrace a positive outlook. Your communication skills are enhancing, and you can easily express yourself clearly and confidently. Your ideas are met with enthusiasm and receptivity from others, opening doors for collaboration.

4 Tuesday

As Jupiter turns direct, a sense of expansion and growth permeates your life. Opportunities previously on hold begin to move forward, and you gain a renewed understanding of faith and optimism in achieving your goals. This transit is a time to embrace the abundance and blessings that come your way and to trust in the universe's support as you journey toward your dreams. The grounding energy of the Taurus Moon brings stability and a deep sense of comfort to your emotions.

5 Wednesday

The cosmic energies now cast a spotlight on your professional endeavors, signaling a time of potential growth and advancement. This phase encourages you to set ambitious yet realistic goals, aligning your career path with your authentic aspirations. Leverage your skills and talents as you navigate the dynamic landscape of work, trusting in cosmic support to guide you toward success and fulfillment.

6 Thursday

As the Moon enters Gemini, a sense of curiosity and mental agility sweeps over you. Your mind becomes sharp and receptive, ready to explore new ideas and engage in stimulating conversations. This transit encourages you to embrace variety, versatility, and the power of communication. You draw social interactions, seeking connections that inspire intellectual growth and exchange. Your ability to multitask heightens, allowing the navigation of different tasks.

7 Friday

Venus sextile Pluto. This aspect invites you to delve into the shadows and uncover hidden truths within yourself and your relationships, leading to profound growth and personal evolution. You can create deep emotional connections that transcend the surface, allowing for greater intimacy and transformation. Trust the process and embrace the transformative power of love Venus sextile Pluto brings into your life.

8 Saturday

As the Moon moves into Cancer, you may feel a deep sense of emotional sensitivity and nurturance. Your focus turns inward, highlighting the importance of creating a safe and comfortable environment for yourself and your loved ones. This lunar transit encourages you to tap into your intuitive and empathetic nature, allowing you to connect with others on a profound emotional level. You may seek solace and comfort in familiar surroundings and the company of loved ones.

9 Sunday

You have the drive, determination, and strategic thinking necessary to take practical steps toward success. You can channel your energy into productive endeavors and make tangible progress. The combination of the Sun conjunct Mercury and Mars trine Saturn creates a dynamic blend of mental understanding, ambition, and discipline, propelling you towards your desired outcomes. Harness this energy to make significant strides and manifest your intentions.

10 Monday

As the Moon enters Leo, your emotions infuse with vibrant and expressive energy. You radiate confidence and a strong sense of self, allowing your inner light to shine brightly. This lunar transit encourages you to embrace your passions, follow your heart's desires, and engage in activities that bring you joy and fulfillment. Your emotions are bold and dramatic, inspiring you to seek out creative outlets and opportunities for self-expression.

11 Tuesday

Sun square Uranus. Be open to embracing the unexpected and finding innovative solutions to any obstacles that come your way. Remember to stay grounded and centered amidst the whirlwind of change, and trust in your ability to adapt and navigate uncertain times. This planetary alignment encourages you to step outside your comfort zone and explore new possibilities, ultimately leading to personal growth and liberation.

12 Wednesday

The Full Moon brings a sense of intensity, urging you to embrace your inner desires and passions. It's an opportune moment to evaluate your progress, celebrate achievements, and make any necessary adjustments to align with your intentions. Pay attention to the messages and revelations that come to light during this time, as they can guide you. Allow the Full Moon's luminous energy to empower you as you navigate your personal growth and transformation journey.

13 Thursday

As the Moon moves into Virgo, you may feel a shift in your focus towards practicality and attention to detail. This transit brings a time of increased organization and efficiency in your daily life. You may find yourself drawn to tasks that require precision and systematic planning. Your analytical abilities heighten, allowing you to identify areas that need improvement and implement practical solutions. Streamline routines and tackle any pending tasks or projects.

14 Friday

Valentine's Day. Mercury ingress Pisces. It's a beautiful opportunity to deepen your emotional bonds, express your love, and engage in heartfelt conversations. Let the energy of Pisces infuse your interactions with tenderness, understanding, and a touch of enchantment. Open your heart and let your words flow with compassion and empathy as you create meaningful connections and celebrate the power of love on this special day.

15 Saturday

Moon ingress Libra is an excellent time to engage in social activities, connect with loved ones, and cultivate a peaceful and harmonious atmosphere in your surroundings. Use this energy to foster compromise, seek diplomatic solutions, and promote fairness in your interactions. The significance of Libra encourages you to find common ground in your interactions. Embrace the beauty of collaboration and the power of the Libra Moon as you navigate the world.

16 Sunday

The celestial currents now guide you toward a phase of introspection, encouraging a deeper connection with your inner self. Take the time to reflect on your journey, allowing the cosmic energies to illuminate the path of self-discovery. Embrace moments of solitude and introspective contemplation, nurturing a profound understanding of your desires, fears, and aspirations. This inward focus brings a sense of clarity, paving the way for a renewed sense of purpose.

17 Monday

You enter clearer skies and can embrace circulating with your wider social environment. Mingling in the community connects you to a refreshing level of abundance. Exchanging thoughts with kindred spirits expands your social life and rejuvenates your soul. News arrives that helps you release the heaviness and transform your vision towards a lighter chapter. A lovely time ahead hits a high note in your social life.

18 Tuesday

As the Sun enters Pisces, you tap into your compassionate and empathetic side. Intuition heightens, and you may find yourself more attuned to the needs and emotions of others. It is a time for connecting with your spiritual essence, embracing creativity, and seeking a deeper understanding of the interconnectedness of all things. Trust in the ebb and flow, and let your intuition guide you toward a more profound sense of self-discovery and spiritual growth.

19 Wednesday

Life takes on a rosy hue when new information crosses your path. It ushers in a time that rekindles your vitality. There is movement ahead in your social life that sparks magic and potential. It brings something to be developed as thoughtful discussions open the trail toward building a unique endeavor. Friends and companions play a role in developing the journey ahead. You land in an environment that is ripe for advancement.

20 Thursday

As the Moon enters Sagittarius and Mercury forms a square aspect with Jupiter, you harness adventure and intellectual expansion. Focus on balancing optimism and practicality, allowing your ideas to flourish while considering the practical implications. Embrace the spirit of Sagittarius by embracing new experiences and learning opportunities. Use the wisdom gained from Mercury's square with Jupiter to navigate conversations and exchanges of ideas with clarity and integrity.

21 Friday

Within the domain of partnerships and relationships, Mars in Cancer adds a layer of emotional assertiveness and protective energy. Feel the assertive tides of Mars guiding your interactions, fostering a sense of passionate commitment and a strong desire to defend those you love. Under this celestial influence, relationships become a cosmic battleground where emotional needs are asserted with passion and sensitivity. Mars invites you to nurture your connections proactively.

22 Saturday

Moon ingress Capricorn. Use this lunar transit to establish a solid foundation for your endeavors, whether in your career, personal life, or any area that requires stability and long-term planning. Embrace the disciplined mindset of Capricorn and tap into your inner strength to overcome obstacles and steadily progress towards your aspirations. With the Moon in Capricorn, you can make significant strides toward your goals and build a solid framework for success.

23 Sunday

In the third house, the Pisces Sun directs its compassionate and imaginative energy toward communication, learning, and local connections. Your approach to information is intuitive, and you may excel in creative and artistic expressions of thought. You find joy in connecting with others through shared imaginative pursuits. Be aware of a potential tendency towards vagueness in communication, and strive to express your ideas with clarity and precision.

24 Monday

As Mars turns direct, a surge of forward-moving energy ignites within you. After a period of introspection and reflection, you're now ready to take action and make progress on your goals. This planetary shift signals a time of increased motivation, assertiveness, and drive. You'll feel a renewed sense of passion and determination, propelling you to overcome obstacles and pursue your desires with vigor. Trust your instincts, harness your inner strength, and embrace the boldness Mars offers.

25 Tuesday

You may find yourself drawn to deep conversations and analytical thinking, seeking practical solutions and strategies for your goals. The combination of Aquarian Moon and Mercury-Saturn conjunction invites you to step outside the box, challenge old beliefs, and approach matters rationally and logically. Embrace this time of mental clarity and innovative thinking to make significant progress in your endeavors and foster meaningful connections with others.

26 Wednesday

You turn a corner and head towards brighter prospects. The future looks rosy as a unique and exciting landscape nurtures new possibilities in your life. You discover a venture that captures the essence of inspiration, enabling you to forge ahead toward developing new projects. An opportunity for collaboration attracts growth and a sense of kinship in your life. It connects with an upbeat time that is lively and engaging.

27 Thursday

You may enter a dreamy and intuitive mind as the Moon enters Pisces. This celestial shift encourages you to tap into your emotional depths, allowing your imagination to soar and your intuition to guide you. You may feel more attuned to the subtle energies and emotions around you, enhancing your empathic abilities. Additionally, the sextile between Mercury and Uranus brings intellectual brilliance to your thoughts and communication.

MARCH

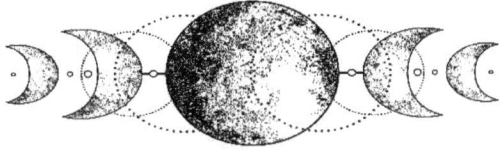

MOON MAGIC

Sun	Mon	Tue	Wed	Thu	Fri	Sat
						1
2	3	4	5	6	7	8
9	10	11	12	13	14	15
16	17	18	19	20	21	22
23	24	25	26	27	28	29
30	31					

NEW MOON

_____

_____

_____

_____

_____

_____

_____

_____

_____

_____

_____

_____

_____

_____

_____

_____

_____

WORM MOON

_____

_____

_____

_____

_____

_____

_____

_____

_____

_____

_____

_____

_____

_____

_____

_____

_____

_____

_____

_____

28 Friday

With the arrival of the New Moon, you discover a fresh start and an opportunity for new beginnings. This lunar phase marks the beginning of a new cycle, urging you to set intentions and plant the seeds of your desires. It is a time of introspection and reflection, where you can align your thoughts and emotions with your goals and aspirations. The energy of the New Moon supports you in manifesting your dreams and creating positive changes in your life.

1 Saturday

With the Moon entering Aries, a fiery and bold energy infuses your emotional landscape. You may feel a surge of passion, courage, and assertiveness, urging you to take action and embrace new beginnings. You're encouraged to trust your instincts, follow your heart's desires, and embark on new adventures. Embrace Aries's confident and pioneering spirit as you step forward with determination and embrace the opportunities that come your way.

2 Sunday

The Sun square Jupiter brings a potential for tensions between expansion and moderation. It encourages you to balance pursuing your aspirations and maintaining a grounded perspective. It's essential to be mindful of excesses and to exercise caution in making grandiose plans. Use this period to reassess your values, gain clarity in your communication, and foster greater self-awareness. Take the opportunity to realign your path with authenticity and wisdom.

3 Monday

Mercury's ingress into Aries makes your thinking more assertive and direct. You feel a surge of mental energy and a desire to take action. It's a time to speak up confidently, assert your ideas, and initiate new projects. As the Moon moves into Taurus, you experience a grounding and stabilizing influence on your emotions. This combination of Mercury in Aries and the Moon in Taurus brings a harmonious balance between boldness and practicality.

4 Tuesday

You can explore paths that heighten abilities; it allows room to evolve into new ways of growth and learning. It brings a journey that is inspiring, trailblazing, and eclectic. Life gets a reboot, taking you towards a chapter of nurturing your talents. Signs and serendipity help guide the path along. Being flexible opens the floodgates to grounding energy that restores balance. A goal comes to life that sparks a shift forward.

5 Wednesday

You can penetrate beneath the surface and uncover concealed truths. You may discover hidden information and make powerful connections. It's an excellent time to dive into intense discussions, explore complex subjects, and bring about transformation through the power of your words. Embrace the energy of the Moon in Gemini and the Mercury sextile Pluto to expand your knowledge, communicate effectively, and delve into the mysteries of life.

6 Thursday

A fortunate trend arrives that takes your vision to a new level. It gives you the green light to merge creativity with tangible results. An energizing influence encourages you to push back the boundaries and take advantage of all offered. Life becomes livelier and more social as you sync up with kindred spirits who understand your take on life. You link up with a happy chapter that opens to new opportunities.

7 Friday

As the Moon moves into Cancer, you may find yourself experiencing a heightened sense of emotional sensitivity and nurturing energy. Your focus turns inward, and you become more attuned to your own needs as well as the needs of those around you. This lunar transit encourages you to create a safe and comforting environment within yourself and your surroundings. You may seek solace in familiar spaces and engage in activities that provide emotional nourishment.

8 Saturday

Sun trine Mars is a harmonious connection that empowers you to assert yourself effectively, maintain your boundaries, and go after what you want with courage and conviction. It's a time of increased passion and courage, where you can tap into your inner strength and accomplish great things. Be mindful of using this energy constructively and responsibly, channeling it into projects and endeavors that align with your highest aspirations.

9 Sunday

Moon ingress Leo is a time to let your light shine brightly and confidently express your passions and talents. Your charisma and enthusiasm attract others to you, and you may find yourself at the center of attention. Use this energy to engage in playful self-expression, pursue your creative endeavors, and connect with others on a heartfelt level. Allow your inner fire to guide you as you embrace this lunar phase in dazzling glory.

10 Monday

Your life is ready to move from strength to strength. A new project ahead offers excitement and sees the fires of your inspiration burn with creativity. It has you focusing on developing a dream goal. A bustling time of expansion draws well-being as life becomes lighter and more energetic. It offers impressive results for your life. It lets you establish grounded foundations that promote a balanced environment around your life.

11 Tuesday

Mercury conjunct Venus alignment enhances your appreciation for beauty, art, and aesthetics. You may find yourself drawn to artistic endeavors or engaging in heartfelt conversations that deepen your connections with others. Use this alignment to express your affection, share your ideas, and foster loving and harmonious relationships. Let the power of words and the beauty of your expression positively impact those around you.

12 Wednesday

As the Moon moves into Virgo, you may experience a sense of practicality and attention to detail. This lunar influence encourages you to focus on organization and efficiency. You may feel a stronger desire to analyze and evaluate situations, seeking practical solutions and taking a systematic approach. The Sun's conjunction with Saturn further amplifies this energy, bringing a sense of discipline and responsibility to the forefront.

13 Thursday

With Mercury and Venus gracing your fourth house, your thoughts, communication, and relationships are deeply influenced by a focus on home and emotional well-being. You have a communicative and affectionate approach to family matters, expressing love and care through open and nurturing conversations. Your home is a place of harmonious communication as you find joy in creating a warm and aesthetically pleasing domestic environment.

14 Friday

During the Full Moon, with the Sun forming a sextile aspect to Uranus and the Moon entering Libra, you are urged to embrace a period of balance, innovation, and self-expression. The Full Moon illuminates your emotions and sheds light on any areas of your life that require harmony and equilibrium. It is a time to find a healthy balance between your personal needs and the needs of others, fostering harmonious relationships and cultivating diplomacy.

15 Saturday

When Mercury turns retrograde, it signifies a time of introspection and reflection. During this period, you may experience delays, miscommunications, or glitches in various areas of your life. It is a valuable opportunity to slow down, reassess your plans, and focus on the details. Take the time to review and revise your projects, relationships, and commitments. It is essential to double-check your work, clarify any misunderstandings, and practice patience in your interactions.

16 Sunday

Within the realm of creativity and self-expression, Uranus in Taurus infuses your artistic pursuits with a cosmic jolt of originality. Feel the innovative energies as Uranus sparks a revolution in your approach to self-expression and creative endeavors. Under this celestial influence, your artistic creations become avant-garde manifestations of your unique individuality, breaking free from traditional norms.

17 Monday

Allow yourself to embrace the transformative energy of Scorpio and engage in self-reflection. It's an influential period for personal growth, healing, and letting go of what no longer serves you. Trust your intuition and navigate through any emotional challenges with courage and resilience. By embracing the intensity of this lunar phase, you can discover hidden aspects of yourself and experience profound transformation.

18 Tuesday

Feel the expansive energy as Jupiter encourages a diversity of tasks and an adaptable approach to your responsibilities. Under this celestial influence, find joy in the variety of your daily endeavors, embracing a flexible mindset that turns challenges into opportunities for growth. Jupiter invites you to infuse your work with a sense of curiosity, transforming the mundane into a cosmic classroom where each task becomes a lesson in expanding your skills and knowledge.

19 Wednesday

When the Moon moves into Sagittarius, it brings a sense of adventure and expansion to your emotional realm. You may feel a longing for new experiences and a desire to explore the world around you. The conjunction of the Sun and Neptune further amplifies this energy, infusing it with dreams, imagination, and spiritual connection. You may find yourself inspired to pursue your aspirations and connect with a more profound sense of purpose.

20 Thursday

As the Sun moves into Aries and the Vernal Equinox heralds the arrival of spring, a surge of energy and vitality infuses your being. You feel a renewed sense of purpose and a desire to take action. It is a time of fresh starts and new beginnings, where you can harness the fiery energy of Aries to pursue your goals and assert yourself in the world. The Vernal Equinox perfectly balances day and night, symbolizing harmony and equilibrium.

21 Friday

When Venus forms a sextile with Pluto, you reveal a potent blend of passion, intensity, and transformation. This aspect brings opportunities for deep emotional connections and profound experiences in your relationships. You may find yourself drawn to explore the depths of your desires and uncover hidden parts of your sensuality. It's a time of magnetic attraction, where you have the potential to create powerful and transformative connections with others.

22 Saturday

Moon ingress Capricorn. You may experience a heightened determination and a desire for achievement. Use this energy to prioritize your responsibilities, set realistic goals, and steadily progress towards them. Remember to balance your emotional well-being with your ambitions, finding ways to nurture and care for yourself while pursuing your objectives. Embrace the Capricorn influence and let it guide you toward a more stable and purposeful emotional state.

23 Sunday

When the Sun is conjunct with Venus, and the Sun is also sextile with Pluto, you may experience powerful and transformative energy in your relationships and personal growth. This alignment brings forth a harmonious blend of love, passion, and inner transformation, empowering you to dive deep into matters of the heart and uncover hidden desires and motivations. You are likely to radiate a magnetic charm that attracts positive attention and opportunities for growth and expansion.

24 Monday

When the Moon ingresses Aquarius and the Sun is conjunct with Mercury, you will likely experience a blend of intellectual stimulation and emotional detachment. Aquarius is an air sign associated with innovation, intellect, and independence. This energy encourages you to embrace your unique perspective and think outside the box. Your mind may be sharp and quick, allowing you to communicate and express yourself with clarity and originality.

25 Tuesday

Mercury sextile Pluto is a good time for research, problem-solving, and seeking information that can empower you intellectually and emotionally. You can transform your thinking patterns and beliefs and engage in meaningful discussions. Harnessing the power of this aspect can help you communicate with authority and influence, making it a good time for negotiations, presentations, and expressing your ideas with conviction.

26 Wednesday

Moon ingress Pisces invites you to explore the depths of emotions and connect with the spiritual dimensions of life. Take moments of solitude to recharge and nourish your soul. Allow the healing energies of Pisces to wash over you, bringing a sense of peace and harmony. Embrace this transit's dreamy and imaginative qualities, and let your imagination soar. Trust your instincts and follow the gentle whispers of your heart as you navigate the ever-changing tides of life.

27 Thursday

When the Black Moon enters Scorpio, and Venus moves into Pisces, a mystical and transformative energy permeates your being. The Black Moon represents the hidden depths and subconscious desires within you, and in Scorpio, it stirs the waters of your soul, inviting you to dive into the shadows and explore the mysteries within. Simultaneously, Venus aligns with Neptune in Pisces, opening the door to boundless love, compassion, and spiritual connection.

28 Friday

Aries, the first sign of the zodiac, ignites your inner spark and propels you forward with confidence and courage. You're motivated to embark on new adventures, set bold goals, and pioneer your path. Trust your instincts and tap into your inner fire as you navigate this energetic and assertive phase. It's an opportunity to embrace your inner warrior and fearlessly pursue your dreams. Let the Moon in Aries fuel your passion and propel you forward with determination and resilience.

29 Saturday

During the New Moon, you can embrace a fresh start and set intentions for the upcoming lunar cycle. This aspect is a time of new beginnings and planting the seeds of your desires. It's a moment to reflect on what you want to manifest in your life and take the necessary steps to realize your dreams. The energy of the New Moon supports your intentions and provides a fertile ground for growth and transformation.

30 Sunday

With Mercury moving into Pisces and joining forces with Neptune, there is a beautiful dance between your thoughts and the realm of dreams. This alignment encourages you to dive deep into your imaginative and creative realms. Your mind becomes a channel, allowing you to tap into the collective consciousness and receive insights that transcend the ordinary. As Neptune enters Aries and the Moon moves into Taurus, a grounding influence anchors these ethereal energies.

APRIL

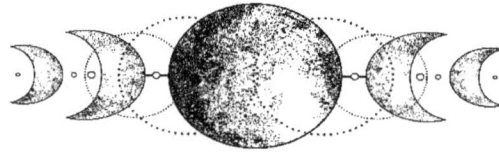

MOON MAGIC

Sun	Mon	Tue	Wed	Thu	Fri	Sat
		1	2	3	4	5
6	7	8	9	10	11	12
13	14	15	16	17	18	19
20	21	22	23	24	25	26
27	28	29	30			

NEW MOON

PINK MOON

31 Monday

Changes ahead keep you on your toes. It transitions you towards a new chapter, and in doing so, you leave outworn aspects of the past behind. It sees motivation returning full force. Life takes on a rosy hue as you create a path that draws abundance. An attractive possibility makes itself known, and it is a powerful lure that takes you out of your comfort zone. It rekindles your vitality and has you feeling motivated to expand your horizons.

1 Tuesday

Moon ingress Gemini. Your emotions may fluctuate more rapidly, reflecting the ever-changing nature of Gemini's influence. It's a time to embrace flexibility and adaptability as you navigate the multiple facets of your thoughts and emotions. Use this lunar phase to express yourself articulately, connect with others through engaging dialogue, and feed your intellectual curiosity. The duality of Gemini allows you to explore new perspectives and communicate with clarity and wit.

2 Wednesday

With the Sun gracing Aries in your fourth house, the cosmic spotlight turns toward home and family life, infusing it with the dynamic and pioneering energy of Aries. Celebrate your roots with courage and assertiveness, embracing a fearless approach to familial bonds. The Sun encourages you to take charge in matters of home and nurture your connections with a bold and confident spirit. Infuse life with warm leadership, creating a home filled with the vibrant energy of Aries.

3 Thursday

Moon ingress Cancer. Your sensitivity heightens, allowing you to empathize and connect with others profoundly emotionally. It's a time to prioritize self-care and emotional well-being, finding solace in life's simple pleasures and cherishing the bonds that bring you a sense of belonging. Trust your instincts and embrace the nurturing energy that Cancer brings, as it invites you to honor your emotions and create a safe space for yourself and those you hold dear.

4 Friday

As Saturn sextiles Uranus and Mars also form a sextile with Uranus, you may experience a harmonious blend of stability and innovation. This combination brings a unique opportunity for you to embrace change while maintaining a solid foundation. You are encouraged to step outside your comfort zone. The alignment of Saturn and Uranus supports you in finding a balance between tradition and progress, allowing you to find creative solutions to challenges.

5 Saturday

The Mars-Saturn trine encourages you to embrace responsibility and take charge of your life. It empowers you to establish a strong work ethic heading toward your objectives. You can harness this harmonious energy to accomplish tasks efficiently, manage time effectively, and demonstrate a mature and focused approach to your endeavors. Remember to balance your drive with patience and resilience, as this trine provides a favorable atmosphere to achieve results.

6 Sunday

As the Moon enters Leo, you may feel confidence and self-assuredness. Your emotions are vibrant, and you are ready to express your authentic self passionately and enthusiastically. The Sun's sextile to Jupiter adds a touch of optimism and expansion to your day, fueling your aspirations and encouraging you to embrace new opportunities. This alignment brings a sense of abundance, allowing you to tap into your natural talents and abilities.

7 Monday

With Venus forming a conjunction with Saturn, you may experience a period of introspection and evaluation in your relationships and values. This alignment brings a sense of seriousness and responsibility to matters of the heart. You might find yourself reassessing your commitments, setting boundaries, and seeking stability and long-term security in your connections. It's a time to take a realistic approach to love, considering both the practical aspects and emotional fulfillment.

8 Tuesday

With Venus forming a sextile aspect of Uranus, you may experience a delightful twist in your relationships and expression. This alignment brings excitement, freedom, and individuality to your interactions and creative endeavors. You may find yourself drawn to unique and unconventional experiences, seeking novelty and spontaneity in your connections. This aspect encourages you to embrace your authentic self and explore new ways of expressing your style and preferences.

9 Wednesday

Unexpected developments open the path wide to new possibilities in your career path. Nurturing this path offers room to progress your abilities to the next level. It draws security as it creates growth and prosperity. It propels your abilities forward and takes your vision to a new level of possibility. This news on the horizon is a morale booster; it sees life shaping up and heading toward an active and productive environment.

10 Thursday

In the workplace, let the celestial energies illuminate your interactions with colleagues. It is a time to expand your knowledge, whether through formal education, self-study, or engaging conversations. Embrace the cosmic guidance that encourages collaboration, effective communication, and a positive work environment. This period invites you to foster cosmic connections with your colleagues, creating a celestial synergy that enhances teamwork and productivity.

11 Friday

The Libra Moon invites you to appreciate the beauty of life and cultivate a sense of aesthetics, seeking out environments that are pleasing to your senses. It is an excellent time to engage in activities promoting balance and facilitating inner harmony. Embrace the diplomatic and peace-loving qualities of the Moon in Libra as you navigate your interactions and create a more balanced and harmonious atmosphere.

12 Saturday

The cosmic muse, Neptune, graces your fifth house, turning the spotlight onto the realm of creativity, romance, and self-expression. Under the celestial glow, let your creative spirit dance to the rhythm of imagination, and allow the waters of Neptune to infuse your love life with a touch of magic. Embrace the dreamlike quality of your passions, transforming the canvas of your expression into a celestial masterpiece painted with the colors of romance and artistic brilliance.

13 Sunday

The Full Moon brings a culmination of energy, illuminating areas of your life that are ready to be acknowledged and released. It's a potent time for reflection, introspection, and emotional transformation. As Venus turns direct, you may experience a shift in your relationships, a renewed sense of clarity, and a deeper understanding of your values and desires. With the Moon entering Scorpio, you explore the depths of your emotions and delve into matters of intimacy and trust.

14 Monday

Embrace the cosmic guidance that encourages collaboration, effective communication, and a positive work environment. This period invites you to foster cosmic connections with your colleagues, creating a celestial synergy that enhances teamwork, innovation, and overall productivity. Allow the celestial currents to guide you in building a cosmic camaraderie that contributes to a harmonious and thriving professional atmosphere.

15 Tuesday

Tune into the celestial cadence of daily life, where the cosmic energies invite you to embrace mindful living. Feel the gentle guidance of the stars as you navigate your routines, fostering balance and intentionality in each activity. It is a time to cultivate habits that nourish both body and spirit, creating a cosmic rhythm that resonates with fulfillment and purpose. Allow the celestial forces to infuse your daily life with a vibrant energy that aligns with your inner cosmic harmony.

16 Wednesday

Today's combination of the Moon in Sagittarius and Mercury in Aries inspires you to speak your truth, take risks, and follow your passions with a fiery determination. It's a time to embrace the excitement of new possibilities and approach life with optimism and spontaneity. Allow the adventurous spirit of Sagittarius and the confident energy of Aries to guide you in pursuing your aspirations and embracing the thrill of the unknown.

17 Thursday

When Mercury forms a conjunction with Neptune, it amplifies your imagination and brings a touch of magic to your thoughts and communication. You may find yourself more attuned to the subtle nuances of language and the hidden meanings behind words. Your intuition heightens, allowing you to tap into a wellspring of creativity and inspiration. However, it's essential to stay grounded and discerning amidst the enchanting influence of Neptune.

18 Friday

Mars ingress Leo. Moon ingress Capricorn. You are willing to put in the necessary effort and work hard to achieve your objectives. This combination encourages you to take charge of your endeavors, assert your authority, and strive for excellence in your chosen path. Embrace the fiery energy of Mars in Leo and the practicality of the Capricorn Moon to make steady progress toward your aspirations, staying focused and determined along the way.

19 Saturday

As the Sun enters the earthy sign of Taurus, you embark on a journey of stability and groundedness. This shift brings a renewed sense of self-worth and a deeper connection with the physical world. You are encouraged to embrace the pleasures of life and indulge in the sensual experiences that bring you joy. Meanwhile, the harmonious trine between Mars and Neptune infuses your actions with a touch of magic and intuition.

20 Sunday

Your words profoundly impact as you inspire and influence others through your insights. With the Moon ingress Aquarius, you feel a strong sense of individuality and a desire to contribute to the collective. A quest for knowledge, innovation, and humanitarian ideals drives you. Embrace the cosmic energy of this day, allowing the harmonious dance of Venus, Mercury, and the Moon to guide you towards personal growth, surprising encounters, and a fresh perspective on life.

21 Monday

In the cosmic dance of celestial energies, the Sun square Mars brings a powerful dynamic to your life. You may find yourself in a position where your desires and ambitions clash with external forces, creating tension and conflict. Be mindful of your actions and reactions during this time, as impulsive or aggressive behavior can arise. Your energy and drive heighten, but channeling them constructively and avoiding unnecessary conflicts is crucial.

22 Tuesday

The stars encourage vibrant interactions and shared experiences. Feel the cosmic currents align as you deepen existing relationships and forge new bonds. It is a period to explore the intricate dance of human connection, allowing the celestial energies to weave threads of understanding and camaraderie within your social sphere. Trust the stars to guide you in fostering authentic connections that contribute to a celestial tapestry of joy and shared experiences.

23 Wednesday

Moon ingress Pisces. Sun square Pluto. Embrace the transformative energy of these aspects and embrace the opportunity to rise above any challenges, cultivating inner strength and resilience. By harnessing the compassionate power of the Pisces Moon, you can navigate the intensity of the Sun square Pluto with grace and wisdom, honoring your emotions while embracing the transformative potential within you.

24 Thursday

Expand your horizons in the cosmic tapestry of personal and spiritual growth. Feel the cosmic winds of change ushering in a transformative phase where the stars encourage you to shed old layers and embrace renewal. Trust in the celestial guidance as you embark on a journey of self-discovery and expansion, allowing the cosmic energies to lead you towards newfound heights of personal and spiritual evolution.

25 Friday

As Venus aligns with Saturn, you may experience a blending of energies that brings a sense of seriousness and responsibility to matters of the heart. This conjunction encourages you to take a practical and disciplined approach to your relationships and how you express your affections. The Moon's ingress into Aries adds a touch of fiery energy and assertiveness to the mix, inspiring you to take action and assert your desires.

26 Saturday

In the realm of creativity and self-expression, the Sun in Taurus ignites a cosmic spark that fuels your artistic endeavors with patience and determination. Your approach to love and romance becomes steadfast and sensual as the Sun bathes the fifth house in the enduring glow of Taurus. This celestial alignment encourages you to express your authentic self with unwavering confidence, appreciating the beauty in both the tangible and the enduring aspects of creative pursuits.

27 Sunday

Embrace the nurturing and patient qualities of the Taurus Moon to cultivate a sense of stability and security within yourself. It's an appropriate period to focus on building a solid foundation and allowing yourself to undergo deep personal transformations that align with your values and bring about positive growth. Stay grounded and trust in the power of this New Moon to initiate fresh starts and guide you toward a path of empowerment and resilience.

MAY

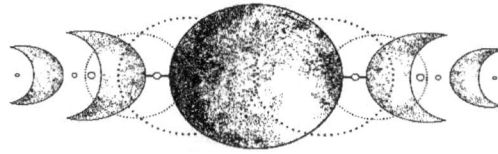

MOON MAGIC

Sun	Mon	Tue	Wed	Thu	Fri	Sat
				1	2	3
4	5	6	7	8	9	10
11	12	13	14	15	16	17
18	19	20	21	22	23	24
25	26	27	28	29	30	31

NEW MOON

FLOWER MOON

_____

_____

_____

_____

_____

_____

_____

_____

_____

_____

_____

_____

_____

_____

_____

_____

_____

_____

_____

_____

_____

28 Monday

Engage with the cosmic energies that converge in the dynamic landscape of business. Let the stars guide you through a period of strategic innovation, urging you to adapt and explore fresh opportunities. Trust the celestial currents to propel you towards success and recognition, fostering a harmonious alignment with your ambitions. In this cosmic dance of entrepreneurship, allow the energy of the stars to illuminate your path and inspire confident strides toward your career goals.

29 Tuesday

Moon ingress Gemini's a time to embrace the power of your words and engage in meaningful dialogue that expands your perspective. Be open to new ideas and opportunities for learning, as the Gemini energy encourages growth and exploration. Stay flexible and adaptable, as your interests and focus may shift rapidly during this lunar phase. Embrace Gemini's playful and social nature, and allow yourself to connect with others through exchanging ideas and thoughts.

30 Wednesday

With Venus ingress Aries, you may feel a surge of passion and assertiveness in your relationships and personal desires. This energy ignites a fiery spark within you, motivating you to pursue your heart's desires with boldness and confidence. You might find yourself drawn to new experiences, seeking excitement and adventure in matters of love and creativity. It's a time to embrace individuality and take the lead in expressing your desires and pursuing what brings you joy.

1 Thursday

Moon ingress Cancer. You may feel a stronger connection to your family, seeking solace and support within the familiarity of your home. This lunar transit encourages you to listen to your intuition and honor your emotions, allowing them to guide you in making decisions that align with your needs and desires. You may find yourself more attuned to the needs of others, offering a compassionate ear and providing a nurturing presence.

MAY

2 Friday

When Venus aligns with Neptune in conjunction, you reveal a world of enchantment and heightened sensitivity. This cosmic combination invites you to explore the depths of your imagination and tap into the realm of dreams and artistic expression. You seek beauty, romance, and a connection to something greater than yourself. It's a time when love and compassion flow effortlessly, inspiring acts of kindness and a desire to connect with others on a soulful level.

3 Saturday

The Leo Moon inspires playfulness, encouraging you to let your inner child roam freely and engage in activities that bring you joy and delight. During this time, you may also feel a strong desire for recognition and appreciation from others, and you have the opportunity to bring warmth and generosity to your interactions. Allow the Leo Moon's radiant energy to ignite your passion and fuel your creative endeavors as you embrace the opportunity to shine in the world around you.

4 Sunday

When Pluto turns retrograde, you may experience a profound inner transformation and introspection. This powerful planetary shift prompts you to delve into the depths of your psyche and explore the hidden realms of your subconscious mind. It's a time of soul-searching and reflection, where you are encouraged to confront your fears, release old patterns, and let go of anything that no longer serves your growth and evolution.

5 Monday

You may desire to improve your daily routines, establish order, and bring a sense of practicality to your life. Harnessing the energy of Mercury sextile Jupiter and the Moon in Virgo, you can make significant progress in your endeavors, expand your horizons, and bring practical wisdom to your decision-making process. Embrace this period as an opportunity to cultivate knowledge, refine your skills, and enhance your overall effectiveness in your personal and professional pursuits.

6 Tuesday

Venus sextile Pluto is an excellent time to delve into matters of the heart, allowing vulnerability and authenticity to guide your interactions. The sextile aspect creates an opportunity for growth, personal evolution, and the potential for positive changes in your relationships. You may find yourself attracted to experiences and connections that hold deep meaning and allow you to tap into the transformative power of love.

7 Wednesday

Embark on a cosmic odyssey of learning and growth where the stars inspire intellectual exploration. It is a time to expand your knowledge, whether through formal education, study, or engaging conversations. Let the celestial energies broaden your horizons, guiding you toward the wisdom that resides in the expansive universe of knowledge. Trust in the cosmic currents to lead you on a journey of continuous learning, fostering personal and intellectual growth.

8 Thursday

Moon ingress Libra. You may find yourself seeking beauty and aesthetics in your surroundings, appreciating art, and engaging in activities that bring peace and tranquility. Use this time to cultivate balance in your life, nurturing both your personal needs and the needs of others. Embrace the energy of Libra as it encourages you to create harmonious connections and foster a sense of peace and cooperation in all aspects of your life.

9 Friday

Dive into the cosmic ocean of inspiration, where the stars illuminate the depths of your creative reservoir. Allow the celestial tides to carry you to uncharted artistic territories, encouraging you to express your unique vision. Like a celestial muse, let the energies inspire waves of creativity that ripple through your creations. It is a period to sail the cosmic seas of imagination, charting a course toward new and boundless artistic horizons.

10 Saturday

As the communicative Mercury enters Taurus, you may notice a shift in your thinking and communication style. Your focus turns towards practicality, stability, and tangible results. Your thoughts become grounded and methodical, seeking practical solutions to challenges. With the Moon moving into Scorpio, your emotions become intense, and you may find yourself drawn towards introspection and self-reflection.

11 Sunday

With Mercury gracing Taurus in your fifth house on Mother's Day, the cosmic storyteller infuses the day with creative and expressive energies. Celebrate the joy of motherhood with heartfelt and artful expressions, whether through innovative projects, heartfelt letters, or playful activities. Mercury in Taurus encourages you to communicate your love tangibly and beautifully, celebrating the unique and artistic qualities of your relationship.

12 Monday

The Full Moon illuminates the shadows, allowing you to see things more clearly and deeply. However, with Mercury square Pluto, there can be intense mental and emotional power struggles. You may reveal challenging thoughts and communication dynamics that require navigating complex emotions and power dynamics. It's essential to approach conversations and interactions with others with patience, empathy, and a willingness to listen.

13 Tuesday

Moon ingress Sagittarius. You are inspired to embark on new adventures, whether it's through travel, learning, or engaging in stimulating conversations with others. The Sagittarius energy encourages you to step out of your comfort zone and embrace the unknown with optimism and enthusiasm. It's a time to connect with your inner wanderer and allow your curiosity to lead the way. Embrace the spirit of adventure and embrace the opportunities that come your way.

14 Wednesday

Feel the cosmic winds of change ushering in a transformative phase where the stars encourage you to shed old layers and embrace renewal. Trust in the celestial guidance as you embark on a journey of self-discovery and expansion, allowing the cosmic energies to lead you towards newfound heights of personal and spiritual evolution. This period invites you to explore the limitless possibilities within, fostering growth on both cosmic and personal scales.

15 Thursday

As the Moon moves into Capricorn, you may notice a shift in your emotional focus towards practicality and ambition. This transit is when you may feel more grounded and determined to achieve your goals. The influence of Capricorn encourages you to take a structured and disciplined approach to your emotions and endeavors. You may find yourself setting clear boundaries and working diligently towards your aspirations.

16 Friday

With Venus gracing Aries in your fourth house, the cosmic artist infuses your home and family life with a spirited and adventurous energy. Celebrate the bonds of kinship with a dynamic and lively approach, injecting excitement into domestic spaces. Venus in Aries encourages you to appreciate the beauty of family dynamics. Home becomes a canvas for vibrant emotions and assertive displays of affection as the flame of Aries ignites the hearth of your familial connections.

17 Saturday

When the Sun aligns with Uranus, you might experience electrifying energy and a sense of liberation. This aspect encourages you to embrace your unique individuality and express yourself authentically. You may feel a strong desire for change and a willingness to break free from old patterns and limitations. You may find yourself drawn to unconventional ideas and people who inspire you to think outside the box.

18 Sunday

The Moon's ingress into Aquarius adds an innovative flavor. You may want to connect with like-minded individuals who share your interests and ideals. Embrace the opportunity to think outside the box and approach challenges uniquely. You can navigate this energetic day with grace and effectiveness by harnessing the positive qualities of both Mercury and Mars, such as clear communication and decisive action while staying open to new ideas.

19 Monday

Ignite the cosmic propulsion of ambition and achievement in your professional sphere. The celestial energies align to guide you through a period of strategic planning and decisive action. Trust in the cosmic currents to propel you towards new heights of success and recognition in your career journey. This journey is a celestial invitation to set audacious goals, seize opportunities, and let the stars be your guiding lights in the expansive universe of your professional aspirations.

20 Tuesday

When the Sun forms a harmonious sextile aspect with Saturn, it brings a sense of stability, discipline, and practicality. This alignment supports your ability to focus, plan, and take responsibility for your actions. You find it easier to establish structure and achieve long-term goals. Your self-discipline and determination heighten, allowing you to tackle tasks and challenges purposefully. With the Moon entering Pisces, your emotions are intuitive, compassionate, and receptive.

21 Wednesday

Immerse yourself in the celestial realm of renewal and healing, where the stars offer a cosmic balm for the soul. Embrace practices that nurture your mind, body, and spirit, fostering a holistic approach to self-care. This period encourages you to bloom and flourish in the garden of your care and nurturing, letting the celestial forces restore balance, vitality, and a sense of overall well-being. Trust in the cosmic energy to guide you on a journey of inner rejuvenation and healing.

22 Thursday

As the Moon enters Aries, you may experience a surge of energy and assertiveness. This ingress is a time of initiating new beginnings, taking decisive action, and embracing adventure. You may feel more courageous and motivated to pursue your goals, and you have the drive to overcome any obstacles that come your way. It's a period of self-discovery and embracing your individuality as you embark on exciting new journeys.

MAY

23 Friday

Immerse yourself in the celestial atelier of artistic expression, where the stars encourage the vibrant hues of creativity to flow freely. Allow your imagination to be the cosmic canvas, painting scenes of innovation and self-expression. Like a celestial muse, the energies inspire you to explore unconventional avenues of creativity, fostering a period of artistic exploration that transcends boundaries and reflects the boundless nature of your creative spirit.

24 Saturday

When the Sun forms a harmonious trine aspect with Pluto, it empowers you to tap into your inner strength and transformational potential. This aspect can bring about positive changes and deep personal empowerment. You may feel more in control of your life and can make powerful choices that align with your true self. With the Moon entering Taurus, you may experience a grounded and stabilizing influence.

25 Sunday

As Saturn enters Aries, you may feel a shift in the energy surrounding your ambitions and responsibilities. Aries is a sign known for its boldness, assertiveness, and pioneering spirit, and with Saturn's influence, you are encouraged to take a disciplined and structured approach to pursue your goals. This transit prompts you to cultivate patience, perseverance, and self-discipline as you navigate new territories and face challenges head-on.

26 Monday

As Mercury enters Gemini, you will likely experience a heightened sense of curiosity and mental agility. Gemini is an air sign known for its intellectual prowess and adaptability. With Mercury, the ruling planet of Gemini, in this sign, your mind will be sharp and receptive to new ideas and information. The sextile aspect between Mercury and Saturn further enhances your ability to focus and organize your thoughts, allowing you to approach tasks efficiently and precisely.

27 Tuesday

During the New Moon, a potent energy of new beginnings and fresh starts fills the air. It's a time when you can set intentions, plant seeds for the future, and embark on transformative journeys. With Mercury trine Pluto, your mind is exceptionally sharp and intuitive, allowing you to delve deep into the mysteries of life and uncover hidden truths. This aspect enables you to communicate with power and conviction, making it a suitable time for research, investigation, and exploration.

28 Wednesday

As the Moon enters Cancer, you may seek to attend to matters of the heart and the nurturing of emotional connections. This lunar ingress brings forth a deep sense of sensitivity and empathy, allowing you to tune into the needs and feelings of those around you. Your intuition heightens, guiding you to seek comfort and security in the familiar and the bonds of family and home. You may feel a stronger desire to create a safe and nurturing environment for yourself and your loved ones.

29 Thursday

With the Sun gracing Gemini in your sixth house, the cosmic luminary illuminates the realm of daily routines and work. Your approach to these aspects of life becomes intellectually charged and adaptable as the energy of Gemini infuses your tasks with versatility. Embrace the joy of mental agility and communication in your work environment, finding satisfaction in areas that allow for diverse thought processes. The Sun in this placement encourages you to shine.

JUNE

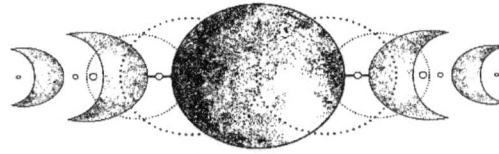

MOON MAGIC

Sun	Mon	Tue	Wed	Thu	Fri	Sat
1	2	3	4	5	6	7
8	9	10	11	12	13	14
15	16	17	18	19	20	21
22	23	24	25	26	27	28
29	30					

New Moon

STRAWBERRY MOON

30 Friday

With the Sun and Mercury aligning, a powerful synergy exists between your thoughts and self-expression. Your mind is sharp, and your communication skills are on point. This transit is when your words carry extra weight and influence, so be mindful of their impact on others. As the Moon moves into Leo, you feel confidence and a desire to shine in the spotlight. Embrace the warmth and enthusiasm of Leo's energy, and let it fuel self-expression and creative endeavors.

31 Saturday

Feel the cosmic currents align as you deepen existing relationships and forge new bonds. Explore the intricate dance of human connection, allowing the celestial energies to weave threads of understanding and camaraderie within your social sphere. Trust the stars to guide you in fostering authentic connections that contribute to a tapestry of joy and shared experiences. Trust in the celestial currents to guide your relationships toward a harmonious and enriching journey.

1 Sunday

As planetary alignments cast their gentle glow on domestic matters, the sanctity of home becomes a focal point. Find solace and fulfillment in the simple pleasures of creating a nurturing environment. Whether you're redecorating, spending quality time with family, or basking in the familiarity of cherished spaces, the celestial energies encourage you to cultivate a sense of warmth and balance within the walls of your abode.

2 Monday

Moon ingress Virgo. Use this energy to streamline your processes and create a sense of order in your daily life. Pay attention to the details and embrace a systematic approach to tasks. This transit is also an excellent time for self-care and nurturing yourself physically and emotionally. Allow the Moon in Virgo to guide you in creating a harmonious and organized environment supporting your well-being.

3 Tuesday

Traverse the cosmic pathways of global awareness and humanitarian endeavors. The stars align to guide your efforts in contributing to the well-being of humanity and the planet. Embrace the celestial energy that encourages compassion, philanthropy, and a commitment to making a positive impact on a global scale. Trust in the cosmic currents to lead you towards a period of meaningful contribution to the greater cosmic community.

4 Wednesday

As the Moon enters Libra, you may seek balance and harmony in your interactions and relationships. You can focus on creating a sense of fairness and cooperation in your interactions with others. You may feel a heightened awareness of the needs and perspectives of those around you and a desire to find common ground and compromise. It is a good time for diplomacy, as you can bring a sense of diplomacy and tact to your communication.

5 Thursday

With Venus sextile Jupiter, you are experiencing a harmonious alignment that boosts positivity and abundance. This aspect enhances social interactions and relationships, fostering a sense of joy, optimism, and generosity. It encourages you to embrace new opportunities for growth and expansion, particularly in areas related to love, creativity, and finances. You may seek out connections that bring mutual benefits and happiness.

6 Friday

When Venus ingresses into Taurus, it brings a grounding and sensual energy to your relationships and an overall sense of beauty and pleasure. This transit encourages you to indulge in simple delights, savor sensory experiences, and find comfort in the material world. You may feel a deeper appreciation for nature, art, and the finer things in life. It's a time to nurture and cultivate your relationships, fostering stability, loyalty, and a sense of security.

7 Saturday

Moon ingress Scorpio transit invites you to embrace the power of vulnerability and trust the wisdom from your emotional depths. It's an opportunity to release what no longer serves you, shed old patterns, and embrace a more authentic and empowered version of yourself. Allow yourself to delve into the mysteries of your psyche and honor the emotional journey that unfolds during this time. Trust your wisdom and allow it to guide you toward growth and healing.

8 Sunday

When Mercury conjuncts Jupiter and ingresses Cancer, you may feel a surge of intellectual and intuitive energy. This alignment enhances your communication skills and expands your mental horizons. It's a time of seeking wisdom, learning, and exploring new ideas. Your mind is receptive to higher knowledge, and you may attract philosophical pursuits. This alignment also brings a nurturing quality to your thoughts and conversations as you express care in your interactions.

9 Monday

When Mercury squares Saturn, you may encounter challenges and obstacles in your communication and thought processes. It can be a time of self-doubt, where you second-guess your ideas and feel restricted. However, this aspect also allows you to strengthen your mental discipline. Embrace the lessons and use them as stepping stones for growth. With the Moon's ingress into Sagittarius, your emotions may be more adventurous and optimistic.

10 Tuesday

Embark on a cosmic journey of craftsmanship and skill where the stars illuminate the path of mastery. This period invites you to hone your talents, embrace creativity, and let the celestial forces guide you toward excellence in your chosen craft. Trust in the cosmic currents as you navigate the constellations of skill development, fostering a period of growth and proficiency in your chosen field. Refinement of abilities cultivates advancement, leading to successful outcomes.

11 Wednesday

During a Full Moon, the lunar energy peaks, illuminating emotions and bringing a sense of culmination. It's a time of heightened awareness and release, allowing you to gain clarity and insights into your emotional landscape. With Mercury sextile Venus, there is a harmonious blend of communication and love. It enhances your ability to express your feelings and desires gracefully. It encourages open and honest conversations, fostering understanding and deeper connections.

12 Thursday

When the Moon ingresses Capricorn, it brings a sense of stability and practicality to your emotions and experiences. You may adopt a more disciplined and focused approach to achieving your goals. This lunar transit encourages you to prioritize responsibilities and work diligently towards your ambitions. You are motivated to establish a solid foundation and take concrete steps toward success. Patience, resilience, and strategic thinking help you harness this transformative energy.

13 Friday

Under the cosmic gaze of Friday the 13th, the energies align to inspire luck and fate. This celestial alignment suggests a day to approach with mindfulness, navigating with a measured and resilient spirit. Embrace the cosmic energies as a guide, finding strength in the shadows and opportunities for growth within the cosmic mysteries that Friday the 13th unveils. This day is a timeless reminder of the heavenly forces which surround your realm.

14 Saturday

As the Moon enters Aquarius, you may feel a shift towards a more independent and intellectually driven mindset. Aquarius is known for its progressive and innovative energy, inspiring you to think outside the box and explore new ideas. During this time, you may crave intellectual stimulation and seek like-minded individuals who share your passions and interests. Embrace your unique perspective and embrace the power of collective thinking.

15 Sunday

When Mars squares Uranus and Jupiter squares Saturn, you experience dynamic and potentially challenging energy. Mars square Uranus can bring unexpected disruptions, sudden changes, and a strong urge for independence and freedom. It's essential to be mindful of impulsive actions and find healthy energy outlets. Meanwhile, Jupiter square Saturn creates a tension between expansion and restriction, as you may encounter obstacles or limitations on your path to growth.

16 Monday

When the Moon ingress Pisces, you are attuned to emotions and the subtle nuances of the world around you. Pisces is a sensitive and intuitive sign, allowing you to tap into your empathetic nature and connect deeply with others. Your imagination soars, and you may find solace in creative or reflective activities. This transit is a time to trust your intuition and go with the flow, allowing your emotions to guide you toward inner growth and spiritual awareness.

17 Tuesday

Mars ingress Virgo's a time to refine your skills, tackle tasks with precision, and seek practical solutions to any challenges. Use this energy to prioritize your well-being, establish effective habits, and progress in your endeavors. You can accomplish your goals efficiently and bring a sense of order and productivity by harnessing Mars in Virgo energy. This transit is an excellent time for planning, organizing, and implementing practical solutions.

18 Wednesday

Moon ingress Aries. Your emotions are more spontaneous and passionate, and you're ready to tackle challenges head-on. You may be eager to start new projects, assert your needs and boundaries, and pursue your goals. Use this energy wisely by channeling it into productive activities, embracing your passions, and taking bold steps toward your aspirations. Trust your instincts and embrace the courage to pursue what sets your soul on fire.

19 Thursday

When Jupiter squares Neptune, you may experience a clash between idealism and reality. Jupiter represents expansion, optimism, and higher knowledge, while Neptune embodies dreams, spirituality, and illusion. This aspect can bring about a sense of confusion or uncertainty as your aspirations and beliefs feel challenged by the practical limitations of the real world. It's essential to be mindful of unrealistic expectations and tendencies to escape from reality.

20 Friday

In the radiant tapestry of celestial energies, your social life takes on an effervescent quality, encouraging you to immerse yourself in the joy of shared experiences and meaningful connections. The cosmos urges you to embrace the beauty of camaraderie. As you navigate the social landscape, allow the cosmic currents to guide you toward a harmonious blend of both lighthearted moments and profound connections, creating a kaleidoscope of laughter and shared adventures.

21 Saturday

Moon ingress Taurus. Sun ingress Cancer. June Solstice. It's a time to honor your emotions, nourish your soul, and create a sense of stability in your life. As the Sun reaches its highest point in the sky, you can also use this time to reflect on your goals and intentions for the coming months. Embrace the energy of this solstice to cultivate a sense of inner peace, emotional well-being, and a strong foundation from which to manifest your desires.

22 Sunday

With Mars forming a harmonious sextile to Jupiter and the Sun in a challenging square aspect with Saturn, you navigate a dynamic interplay of energy. The Mars-Jupiter sextile boosts confidence, enthusiasm, and an eagerness to take action toward your goals. It fuels your motivation and encourages you to expand your horizons, embracing opportunities for success. However, the Sun-Saturn square presents some obstacles that require attention.

23 Monday

Moon ingress Gemini. Sun square Neptune. Take extra care in communication, and ensure you express yourself clearly and honestly. It is a time to be discerning and maintain a healthy skepticism while tapping into your intuition and seeking more profound insights. By remaining adaptable and open-minded, you can navigate the nebulous energy of the Sun square Neptune and embrace the intellectual and communicative opportunities that the Moon in Gemini brings.

24 Tuesday

Sun conjunct Jupiter alignment brings positive energy, enthusiasm, and a belief in your abilities. It's a time to embrace optimism, embrace new possibilities, and seize the opportunities that come your way. Allow the Sun-Jupiter conjunction to ignite your spirit and propel you towards a brighter and more fulfilling future. Embrace the abundance surrounding you, and let your inner light shine, inspiring others to join your cosmic dance.

25 Wednesday

With the Moon transitioning into Cancer and the arrival of the New Moon, you are invited to embrace a period of emotional renewal and fresh beginnings. The nurturing energy of Cancer infuses your being, encouraging you to connect with your emotions and create a sense of comfort and security in your life. It is a time to set intentions and plant the seeds of new beginnings, as the New Moon signifies a fresh chapter in your journey.

26 Thursday

The Sun-Mars sextile fuels your motivation and drive, empowering you to take action and pursue your goals with determination. As Mercury enters Leo, your communication style becomes bold and expressive. You can captivate others with your words and convey your ideas with passion. Embrace this energy and let your creativity shine. Trust your abilities and let your thoughts and actions shape a bright and inspiring path.

27 Friday

With the Moon transitioning into Leo, you hum with vibrant and expressive energy. Embrace your inner light and shine brightly in all that you do. The Leo Moon encourages you to tap into your creativity, passion, and self-confidence. It invites you to enter the spotlight and share your unique gifts and talents with the world. Allow your authentic self to be seen and heard, and let your creativity flow freely. It is a time to indulge in activities that bring you joy and ignite your passion.

28 Saturday

Mercury trine Saturn. Mercury trine Neptune. Your communication style is thoughtful, wise, and infused with a touch of magic. You can convey complex concepts in a way that is easily understood and resonates with others deeply. Use this powerful energy to manifest your dreams and realize your visions. Trust in your intuition and let your words be a vessel for inspiration and transformation. It's a favorable time to plan, organize, and realize your visions.

29 Sunday

The opposition between Mercury and Pluto brings intensity and depth to your mental processes. It can uncover hidden truths and reveal underlying power dynamics in your thinking patterns. It can lead to intense debates, mental obsessions, or a tendency to be overly critical of yourself and others. Meanwhile, the Moon's ingress into Virgo adds a practical and analytical touch to your emotional landscape.

JULY

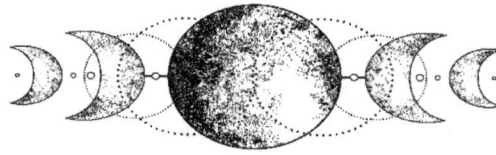

MOON MAGIC

Sun	Mon	Tue	Wed	Thu	Fri	Sat
		1	2	3	4	5
6	7	8	9	10	11	12
13	14	15	16	17	18	19
20	21	22	23	24	25	26
27	28	29	30	31		

CAPRICORN

New Moon

BUCK MOON

_____

_____

_____

_____

_____

_____

_____

_____

_____

_____

_____

_____

_____

_____

_____

_____

_____

_____

_____

30 Monday

Step into the cosmic dawn of personal transformation, where the celestial energies encourage you to shed old skins and embrace renewal. Let the stars be your guiding forces as you navigate the transformative currents, fostering a period of self-discovery and evolution. This cosmic journey invites you to align with your authentic self, trusting in the celestial guidance to lead you towards newfound heights of personal growth and empowerment.

1 Tuesday

The influence of Libra Moon brings an awareness of aesthetics and a desire for beauty and elegance in your surroundings. You may appreciate art, music, and the finer things in life. Nurturing your social connections during this time is essential, as Libra is a sign associated with partnerships and friendships. Focus on maintaining a sense of fairness and diplomacy in your interactions, and use your natural charm and tact to navigate any challenges that may arise.

2 Wednesday

With Mars in Virgo influencing your ninth house, your energy and assertiveness are directed toward intellectual pursuits, travel, and expansive goals. You approach life with a practical and strategic mindset, often seeking to broaden your horizons through education or cultural experiences. Your assertiveness may manifest in advocating for your beliefs or engaging in philosophical debates. Strive to channel your dynamic energy into constructive and open-minded perspectives.

3 Thursday

Enter the celestial realm of innovation and technology, where the stars align to guide your ventures into the digital cosmos. This cosmic period encourages you to explore cutting-edge ideas, embrace technological advancements, and let the celestial forces be the guiding constellations in your pursuit of groundbreaking innovations. Trust in the cosmic currents to propel you towards new horizons in the ever-expanding universe of technological possibilities.

4 Friday

With Venus conjunct Uranus and Venus ingress Gemini, unexpected and exciting changes may arise in your relationships and love life. You may crave unique and unconventional connections, seeking freedom and novelty in your interactions. It can be a time of liberation and exploration as you express your desires authentically. As Neptune turns retrograde, you are encouraged to reflect on your dreams, ideals, and spiritual path.

5 Saturday

Within the realm of partnerships and relationships, the Sun in Cancer adds a nurturing touch to your interactions. Your approach to connections becomes rooted in emotional support and familial bonds, as Cancer's energy encourages you to create a nurturing space for your relationships to flourish. Embrace the joy of forming deep emotional connections with others, celebrating the beauty of shared emotions and the comfort of a protective and caring partnership.

6 Sunday

With the Moon moving into Sagittarius, you may feel a renewed sense of adventure and a desire to explore new horizons. This transit encourages you to embrace your curiosity, expand your horizons, and seek experiences that broaden your perspective. It's a time of growth, optimism, and a renewed zest for life. Embrace the opportunities for development and connection that come your way, and trust in the power of love and your inner wisdom.

7 Monday

When Uranus enters Gemini, you may experience a wave of intellectual and communicative energy. This transit encourages you to embrace change and explore new ideas and perspectives. Your mind becomes open and receptive to innovative concepts, and you may draw unconventional approaches in various areas of your life. Venus forms a trine with Pluto, bringing powerful and transformative energy to your relationships and personal desires.

8 Tuesday

The Sun in Cancer adds a nurturing and protective quality to your interactions. In your professional relationships, you shine brightest when you approach collaborations with a genuine concern for the emotional well-being of your partners. The Sun in this placement encourages you to create a supportive and familial atmosphere in your work partnerships, fostering a sense of security and shared emotional values.

9 Wednesday

With the Moon entering Capricorn, you may feel a stronger sense of determination and ambition in your emotional landscape. It is a time for setting practical goals and taking steps towards achieving them. You may focus more on your responsibilities and commitments, seeking stability and structure. It's an opportunity to tap into your discipline and work ethic, using them to make progress in areas that are important to you.

10 Thursday

The Full Moon invites you to embrace your emotions, honor your feelings, and seek balance within yourself and your relationships. Use this time to gain clarity, set intentions, and take inspired action toward your goals. Allow the Full Moon energy to guide you in expressing your authentic self and embracing your inner power. Trust in the process, surrender to the cosmic energies, and embrace the opportunities for growth and expansion that the Full Moon brings.

11 Friday

Moon ingress Aquarius. Use this energy to engage in stimulating conversations, expand your social circle, and seek new experiences that broaden your horizons. The Moon in Aquarius encourages you to embrace your inner rebel and the power of collective change. Allow your mind to wander, explore new ideas, and think outside the box. Embrace the freedom to be authentic and let your individuality shine brightly.

12 Saturday

Within the cosmic symphony, your daily routine becomes a canvas for mindful living. Planetary influences inspire you to streamline tasks, infusing your day-to-day life with a sense of efficiency and purpose. Embrace rituals that contribute to your overall well-being, fostering a harmonious rhythm that allows you to navigate each day with intentionality. The celestial energies guide you towards a balanced approach that contributes to a fulfilling and rewarding daily existence.

13 Sunday

Saturn turns retrograde. Moon ingress Pisces. This combination encourages you to balance practicality and intuition, allowing you to navigate the depths of your emotions while also honoring your responsibilities. Use this time to delve into your subconscious, gain insights, and make necessary adjustments to create a solid foundation for personal growth. Trust your inner wisdom and seek support from your intuition as you navigate the ebb and flow of life.

14 Monday

Good news ahead brings a significant shift forward that teams you up with rising prospects. It offers an uptick of new options that have you feeling energized and ready to tackle new projects with a view toward advancement. You discover a unique opportunity that captures the essence of inspiration and enables you to build grounded foundations that offer room to improve your home and work life. It brings inspiration and heightened security.

15 Tuesday

With Venus in Gemini in the sixth house, your approach to work, daily routines, and health is marked by a need for communication, flexibility, and intellectual engagement. You find pleasure in a harmonious and friendly work environment, and your creative energy may thrive in roles that involve communication or variety. Health routines may be approached with a desire for diversity and mental stimulation, such as engaging in different forms of exercise or wellness practices.

16 Wednesday

When the Moon enters Aries, you may feel a surge of energy and enthusiasm. This fiery and assertive energy ignites your passion and drive, encouraging you to take bold action and pursue your goals with determination. You may experience a sense of renewed vitality and a desire for new beginnings. It's a time to trust your instincts and embrace your inner warrior. Use this energy to initiate projects, tackle challenges, and assert individuality.

17 Thursday

Significant change brings a chapter that empowers and enriches your life. Being proactive draws a pleasing result as swift improvements follow the expansion of horizons around your life. You ramp up the potential possible by being flexible and adaptive to change. Communication arrives that shines the light around deepening friendships. An opportunity for collaboration offers growth and a sense of kinship.

18 Friday

With Mercury sextile Venus, you can enhance your communication skills and express yourself with grace and charm. Take advantage of this alignment to strengthen your connections with others and find harmony in your interactions. Embrace the Mercury retrograde energy by revisiting creative projects or reconnecting with old friends. Be patient and adaptable; this period offers valuable insights and opportunities to realign your intentions and goals.

19 Saturday

With Mercury in Leo in the eighth house, your thoughts and communication style are directed toward matters of intimacy, shared resources, and transformation. You approach discussions on deep and meaningful topics with passion and conviction. Your expressive nature may shine in roles involving research, investigation, or uncovering truths. Strive for open dialogue to foster emotional connections and transformative experiences in your relationships and pursuits.

20 Sunday

When the Moon moves into Gemini, you may feel a shift in your emotional energy. This transit is a time of curiosity, adaptability, and mental agility. You may be more open to new ideas and eager to engage in stimulating conversations. Your mind is quick and receptive, allowing you to absorb information and make connections effortlessly. It's a favorable time for learning, networking, and exploring different perspectives.

21 Monday

Resources and support help you get busy manifesting your vision. The benefits ahead bring something to celebrate. It does bring the curtain up on a fresh chapter that places you center stage to improve your world. It provides a creative aspect that draws communication, ideas, and brainstorming sessions. Supportive energy brings a considerable boost to your life as the possibility of new assignments glimmers overhead.

22 Tuesday

Moon ingress Cancer. Sun ingress Leo. This combination of energies invites you to connect with your inner self, express your authentic emotions, and let your creative light shine. Allow yourself to indulge in joyful activities and pursue endeavors that bring you happiness and fulfillment. Embrace your inner child and play, create, and express yourself passionately. Remember to balance your emotional needs with the desire for self-expression, finding a harmonious blend.

23 Wednesday

As the Sun forms a harmonious sextile with Uranus, you may feel excitement and a desire for change and innovation. This aspect encourages you to embrace your unique individuality and explore new possibilities. It's a time to break free from routine and embrace your authentic self, allowing your true passions and talents to shine. However, the square between Venus and Mars may create tension in relationships and desires.

24 Thursday

With the New Moon, a fresh start allows you to set new intentions, plant seeds of manifestation, and embark on a journey of personal transformation. It is a powerful time to align your inner desires with your outer actions and manifest your dreams into reality. Embrace the harmonious energy of the Sun trine Saturn and Sun trine Neptune, combined with the confident and radiant power of the Moon in Leo, to create a life of purpose, creativity, and spiritual fulfillment.

25 Friday

Sun-opposed Pluto aspect challenges you to confront your deepest fears, hidden desires, and power dynamics. It urges you to examine the areas where you may resist change or hold onto control. You may experience power struggles or confrontations that force you to reassess your boundaries and assert your authenticity. It is a time of self-discovery and inner transformation, where you can release old patterns and embrace your power.

26 Saturday

Moon ingress Virgo energy encourages you to analyze and refine your routines, seeking improvement and effectiveness. You might find satisfaction in taking care of practical tasks, tending to your health and well-being, and creating a harmonious environment. The Moon in Virgo brings a sense of practicality and a willingness to try to achieve your goals. It's a time to be attentive to the small things and find joy in caring for yourself and your responsibilities.

27 Sunday

The celestial canvas invites you to explore the depths of your imagination, encouraging self-expression through various artistic mediums. Whether embarking on a passion project, engaging in a creative collaboration, or indulging in a cherished hobby, the cosmic energies inspire you to tap into your inventive side. Infuse your daily life with a touch of artistic flair, allowing the vibrant hues of creativity to paint your existence with beauty, inspiration, and self-discovery.

28 Monday

As you create a bridge towards growing your dreams, you discover a venture that opens the door wide. Essential information flows into your life. It brings news that helps you turn a corner and head towards growth. It marks a path of abundance that brings security and balance to your foundations. Being open to new options lets you transition towards rising prospects as you advance in life and gain traction on growing your vision.

29 Tuesday

As the Moon moves into Libra, you may experience a shift towards a more harmonious and balanced emotional state. This transit encourages you to seek harmony and fairness in your relationships and interactions with others. You might feel more empathetic and understanding of different perspectives, which can lead to smoother communication and cooperation. It is a favorable time to engage in social activities, connect with friends, and build bridges with others.

30 Wednesday

You can appreciate the events on the horizon as they bring new information. It gives you an open road to developing dreams and a journey towards advancement. Nurturing your talents extends your reach into unique areas worth investing time and energy in. Your situation is evolving, bringing opportunities to share your expertise. Opportunity comes knocking and carries an exciting sign that things are shifting forward.

31 Thursday

Venus ingress Cancer transit can bring nurturing and caring energy, making you more attuned to the needs and feelings of others. You may prioritize creating a comfortable and safe home environment where you can express your emotions freely and find solace. The Moon entering Scorpio enhances your emotional intensity and depth, encouraging you to delve into your inner world and uncover hidden feelings and desires.

AUGUST

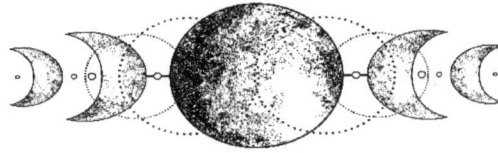

MOON MAGIC

Sun	Mon	Tue	Wed	Thu	Fri	Sat
					1	2
3	4	5	6	7	8	9
10	11	12	13	14	15	16
17	18	19	20	21	22	23
24	25	26	27	28	29	30
31						

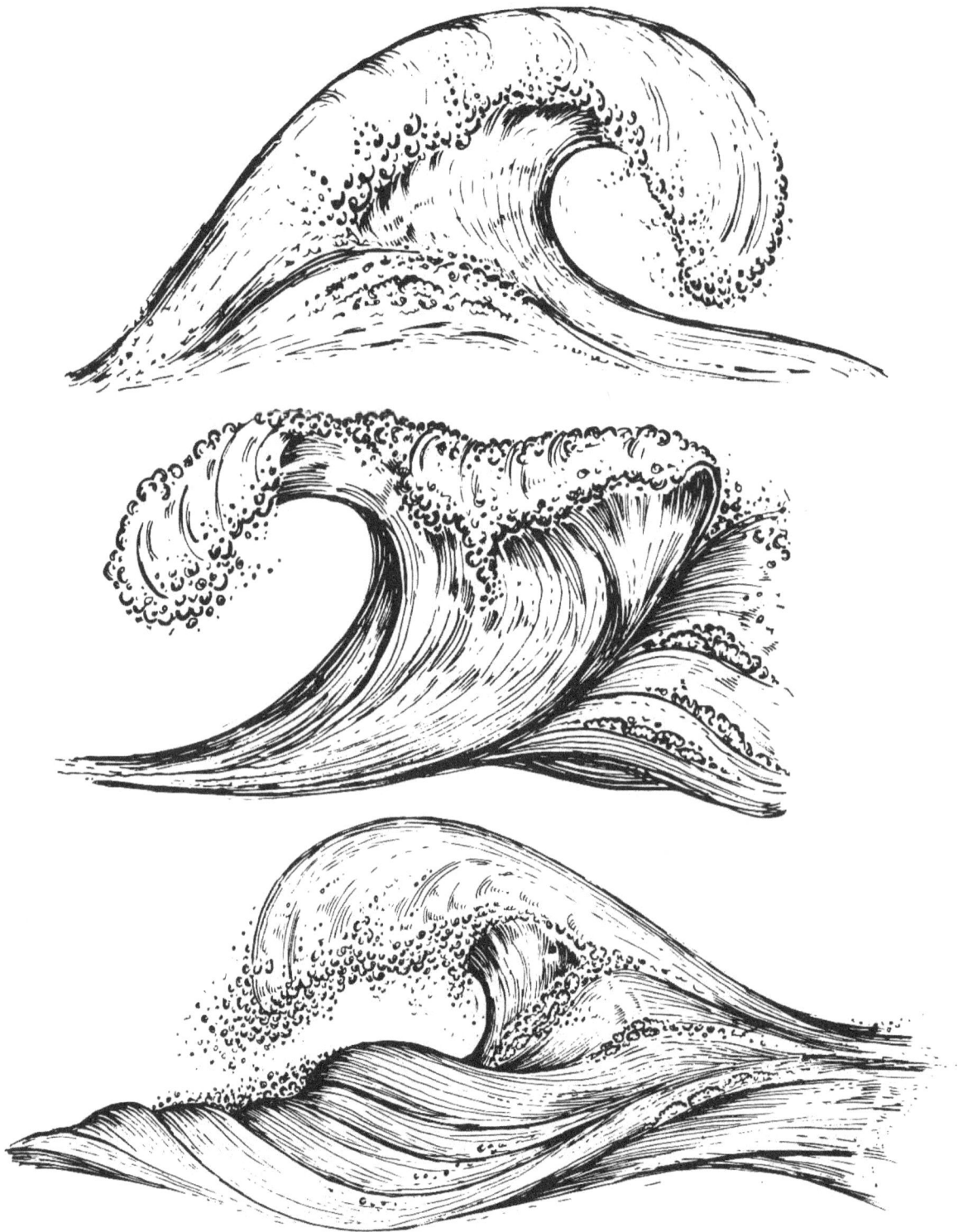

NEW MOON

STURGEON MOON

1 Friday

When Venus forms a square with Saturn and Neptune, you may experience challenges and tensions in your relationships and personal desires. Saturn's influence might bring feelings of restriction or limitation in love and self-expression, leading you to reassess your values and commitments. It's essential to be patient and realistic about your expectations. Take the opportunity to reflect on your needs and boundaries, making sure expectations are realistic and grounded.

2 Saturday

In the intense and mysterious eighth house, your Leo Sun infuses your life with passion and depth. You approach shared resources and intimate connections with a dramatic flair, seeking intensity and transformation. A desire for growth may mark your financial endeavors for recognition and success, but it's crucial to navigate these waters with honesty and integrity. Be mindful of power dynamics in intimate relationships, striving for authenticity and mutual empowerment.

3 Sunday

As the Moon moves into Sagittarius, you might experience a sense of adventure and a craving for new experiences. This cosmic transit is when you may feel more optimistic and enthusiastic about life. Your mind could draw broader horizons and philosophical ideas, and you may seek knowledge and wisdom. Embrace this period to explore new perspectives and embark on journeys, whether they are physical or intellectual.

AUGUST

4 Monday

Navigate the celestial pathways of self-advancement, where the emphasis on uplifting your situation draws an inspiring trajectory into your life. Rising prospects on the cosmic horizon reveal the secret code to expanding your existence. Embrace a fresh approach that propels momentum into your world, and as the cosmic rhythm quickens, bask in the uplifting results that materialize from your proactive strides.

5 Tuesday

With the Moon moving into Capricorn, you may notice a shift towards a more structured and disciplined approach to your emotions and goals. This transit encourages you to take a practical and responsible stance, prioritizing long-term achievements and stability. You might feel determined to tackle tasks and challenges with a vital purpose. Staying focused and organized is essential, making the most of your time and energy.

6 Wednesday

As Mars moves into Libra, you may experience a shift in how you assert yourself and take action. This transit encourages you to find a balanced and harmonious approach to interacting with others. You might feel more diplomatic and considerate, seeking compromises and fair solutions to conflicts. Use this time to strengthen your relationships and partnerships, as Mars in Libra fosters cooperation and teamwork.

7 Thursday

You are ready to open the floodgates and embrace a brighter chapter. Being open to growing your circle of friends lets you adopt a journey that captures the essence of inspiration. It marks a freedom-driven time that brings a more social environment that tempts you out and about. Engaging with a broader world of potential brings a refreshing change of pace to your life. An invitation ahead carries you forward on the winds of change.

8 Friday

With the Moon moving into Aquarius and forming a harmonious trine with Uranus, you may feel the excitement and an urge to embrace your individuality. This astrological combination encourages you to break free from routines and explore new and innovative ways of expressing yourself. You might find yourself drawn to unconventional ideas or seeking unique experiences that stimulate your mind and spark your creativity.

9 Saturday

With Mars forming oppositions to Saturn and Neptune during this Full Moon, you might experience internal conflicts and challenges. You may feel a strong drive and ambition to pursue your goals and assert yourself. However, Saturn's influence might bring obstacles and delays that test your patience and determination. Staying disciplined and focused is crucial, as well as balancing taking action and being cautious.

10 Sunday

With the Moon entering Pisces and Mars forming a harmonious trine with Pluto, you may find yourself experiencing a mix of emotions and increased intensity in your actions. The Moon in Pisces can enhance your sensitivity and compassion, making you more attuned to the needs of others. Connect with your intuition and engage in creative pursuits that fulfill your soul. With Mars trine Pluto, your energy and drive allow you to pursue your goals with determination and purpose.

11 Monday

Mercury turns direct. You might notice a renewed focus and efficiency in your daily tasks and communication with others. Take advantage of this forward momentum to make progress in areas on hold, and use this time to express yourself with greater ease and effectiveness. Remember that while Mercury is now direct, it's still important to remain attentive to the details and practice patience as the energy of this transition settles in.

12 Tuesday

Saturn sextiles Uranus, and a harmonious blend of stability and innovation emerges. This aspect encourages you to find creative ways to incorporate new ideas and progressive changes while maintaining a solid foundation and structure. It's an excellent time to make practical adjustments that align with your long-term goals and aspirations. With Venus conjunct with Jupiter, an air of positivity and abundance surrounds your relationships and financial matters.

13 Wednesday

In the professional realm, the cosmic stage is set for the alignment of your ambitions with a profound sense of purpose. Whether you find yourself advancing in your current role or exploring new career paths, the celestial energies support your journey toward professional fulfillment. It is a time to harness your unique skills and talents, trusting cosmic guidance as you navigate the dynamic landscape of work.

14 Thursday

Moon ingress Taurus transit encourages you to focus on life's practical aspects and find comfort in the familiar. It's a favorable time to indulge in self-care and pampering, nurturing yourself with soothing activities and simple pleasures. You may find that you're more in tune with your senses and attuned to the beauty around you. This phase also focuses on financial matters, prompting you to assess and manage your resources wisely.

15 Friday

With Mercury sextile Mars, you may experience a boost in your mental energy and communication skills. This harmonious aspect encourages clear and assertive communication, making expressing your ideas and opinions easier. Your mind is sharp and focused, allowing you to tackle tasks and projects with enthusiasm and efficiency. It's a great time to engage in debates or discussions, as you will likely be quick-witted and persuasive.

16 Saturday

With the Moon ingressing Gemini, you might feel more curious, adaptable, and social. Your mind is buzzing with ideas and interests, and you are eager to engage in various conversations and activities. It is a great time to connect, exchange thoughts, and learn something new. You may feel more communicative and open to exploring different perspectives. Embrace the versatility of this lunar energy and use it to enjoy the diversity life has to offer.

17 Sunday

With Venus in Cancer in the seventh house, your approach to partnerships, relationships, and one-on-one connections is marked by emotional depth, nurturance, and a desire for security. You express love and affection openly in your relationships, valuing a solid emotional connection with your partner. Your home and family life are likely to play a significant role in your romantic pursuits, and you may seek a partner who shares your nurturing values.

18 Monday

As Mercury forms a sextile with Mars, you may find that your communication skills heighten, allowing you to express your ideas with assertiveness and precision. This harmonious aspect encourages dynamic thinking and quick decision-making, empowering you to take action on your plans and goals. Meanwhile, with the Moon's ingress into Cancer, your emotions may become more pronounced, fostering a sense of sensitivity and nurturing within you.

19 Tuesday

Immerse yourself in the cosmic garden of personal growth, as the emphasis on improving your circumstances sets the stage for an inspiring journey. Prospects ascend like cosmic blooms, revealing the secret code that unlocks new dimensions of life's expansion. Discover a novel approach that breathes momentum into your reality, and as the cadence of life accelerates, find solace in the uplifting results that accompany your proactive endeavors.

20 Wednesday

As the Moon enters the fiery sign of Leo, you can expect a boost of creativity and self-expression in your life. This celestial shift infuses you with confidence and charisma, making it a great time to shine in social settings and showcase your unique talents; your warmth, affection, and positive energy inspire and uplift. You might find yourself seeking more attention and recognition, and that's perfectly fine – embrace the spotlight and let your inner light radiate brightly.

21 Thursday

Embark on a cosmic expedition centered on uplifting your circumstances, cracking the code to unlock a myriad of opportunities. The prospect of an expansive life becomes tangible as you navigate the celestial currents. A newfound approach gathers momentum, infusing vitality into your existence. Feel the acceleration of life's rhythm, a cosmic dance that resonates with encouraging outcomes and propels you toward a brighter horizon.

22 Friday

Sun ingress Virgo. Your ability to plan and strategize heightens, and you might find yourself drawn to improving your daily routines and adopting healthier habits, as the Virgo energy inspires a desire for self-improvement. It is an opportune moment to set goals and work toward achieving them step by step. Embrace the Earth element's grounding influence, and let your logical and systematic approach guide this increased productivity and growth period.

23 Saturday

The New Moon canvas invites you to explore the kaleidoscope of creativity within your soul. Embrace the liberating energy surrounding your artistic pursuits, allowing your imagination to unfurl in vibrant hues. Whether through traditional arts, innovative projects, or collaborative ventures, let the cosmic forces inspire you to tap into your creative wellspring. This period encourages you to dance with inspiration, fostering a playful and curious approach to your creative endeavors.

24 Sunday

Sun square Uranus. The celestial architects craft a chapter of stability and growth within your home life. As the cosmic forces align, consider making subtle adjustments to your living space or establishing new rituals that enhance domestic harmony. It is a time to create a sanctuary that nurtures your well-being, fostering a sense of security and inspiration. Allow the cosmic energy to guide you in transforming your home into a haven of comfort and positive energy.

25 Monday

With Venus also moving into Leo, there's an added flair of creativity, passion, and self-expression in your romantic endeavors and personal pursuits. You may feel a stronger desire for affection and appreciation, which could lead to moments of grand gestures and warm displays of love. Embrace the playful and generous qualities of Venus in Leo to add excitement and joy to your connections with others.

26 Tuesday

With Venus forming harmonious trines to Saturn and Neptune and a sextile to Uranus, you may experience positive and uplifting energy in your relationships and creative endeavors. The trine to Saturn brings stability and a sense of commitment to your romantic connections and artistic pursuits. You might find that your efforts to build lasting and meaningful bonds are supported, and your dedication to your craft is recognized and rewarded.

27 Wednesday

With Venus opposing Pluto, you may experience intense emotions and power struggles. This astrological aspect can bring hidden desires, jealousy, and control issues to the surface. You might find yourself drawn to situations or people that evoke strong feelings, but it's crucial to be cautious and avoid getting entangled in manipulative dynamics. This period can be transformative, encouraging you to confront deep-seated love, trust, and attachment issues.

28 Thursday

Moon ingress Scorpio. This lunar transit brings about a time of introspection and a willingness to explore the deeper aspects of your psyche. You might find yourself drawn to mystery, hidden truths, and the esoteric, seeking to uncover the underlying motivations behind your feelings and actions. Scorpio's energy is passionate and transformative, inviting you to release any emotional baggage and embrace personal growth.

29 Friday

Uranus sextile Neptune. This harmonious alignment of these two planets can bring about a sense of innovation and a deeper understanding of the world around you. Your imagination is activated, and you may crave new and unconventional ideas. This transit is when your creative and spiritual faculties are aligned, allowing you to tap into higher realms of consciousness and connect with a broader perspective.

30 Saturday

Moon ingress Sagittarius lunar transit brings expansive energy that encourages you to seek new experiences, broaden your horizons, and embrace a more adventurous outlook. You might seek to learn, travel, or explore different cultures and belief systems. Sagittarius' influence can inspire you to express your thoughts and emotions openly and enthusiastically, making it a favorable time for open discussions and sharing ideas.

31 Sunday

The celestial choreographer directs a symphony of connection within your relationships, inviting you to harmonize with the cosmic melodies of shared experiences. Explore the intricate dance of human connection, whether through heart-to-heart conversations, collaborative projects, or shared adventures. Feel the magnetic pull of celestial forces as you deepen bonds, fostering a sense of unity and joy in the cosmic dance of your social life.

SEPTEMBER

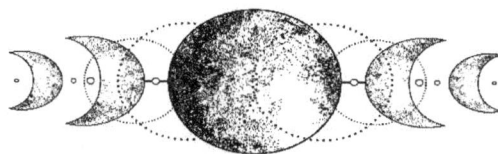

MOON MAGIC

Sun	Mon	Tue	Wed	Thu	Fri	Sat
	1	2	3	4	5	6
7	8	9	10	11	12	13
14	15	16	17	18	19	20
21	22	23	24	25	26	27
28	29	30				

NEW MOON

Corn/Harvest Moon

September

1 Monday

Your intuition and emotional intelligence heighten, allowing you to navigate complex situations gracefully and wisely. Saturn's presence in Pisces also calls for a deeper connection to your spiritual self and a willingness to explore matters beyond the material realm. It's a time to set realistic boundaries and work towards emotional maturity and personal growth. Embrace this transit's introspective and intuitive qualities, which can lead you to a deeper understanding.

2 Tuesday

As the Moon enters Capricorn, you might feel a sense of increased responsibility and a focus on achieving your goals. This lunar transit encourages you to adopt a disciplined approach to your emotions and endeavors. You may find yourself setting clear intentions and working diligently to accomplish them. With Mercury also moving into Virgo, your communication style becomes precise and detail-oriented. You excel in organizing thoughts and expressing them with clarity.

3 Wednesday

Mercury square Uranus' astrological influence can bring sudden insights and innovative ideas but can also lead to mental agitation and impulsiveness. You may find your mind racing with new information and unconventional thoughts, making it challenging to concentrate on one thing for too long. It's essential to stay open to new perspectives and be mindful of impulsive decision-making and potential conflicts arising from misunderstandings.

4 Thursday

As the Moon enters Aquarius, you might notice a shift in your emotional energy towards a more open and progressive outlook. Aquarius' influence encourages you to embrace your uniqueness and individuality, fostering a sense of belonging to a broader community of like-minded individuals. You may be more interested in humanitarian causes and social activities promoting positive change during this lunar transition.

5 Friday

With Mars forming a square aspect to Jupiter, you might experience a surge of enthusiasm and confidence that can lead to ambitious pursuits. This astrological influence can amplify your desires for growth and achievement, urging you to take on challenges and expand your horizons. However, it's essential to be mindful of overextending yourself or taking on too much, as the combination of Mars and Jupiter can lead to excessive optimism and impulsiveness.

6 Saturday

As Uranus turns retrograde, you may feel a shift in your external and internal landscape. This planetary event can bring a sense of introspection and a desire to reevaluate your approach to change and independence. You might reflect on past experiences and seek a deeper understanding of individuality. It's a time to break free from stagnant patterns and embrace a period of self-discovery and personal growth.

7 Sunday

The Full Moon represents a time of completion and illumination, as the Sun and Moon oppose each other, bringing to light any imbalances or unresolved issues. You might feel a surge of energy and heightened awareness, prompting you to take stock of your achievements and challenges since the New Moon. This cosmic aspect is an ideal time to release what no longer serves you and embrace a renewed sense of purpose.

8 Monday

As the Moon enters Aries, you may feel energy and assertiveness in your emotional landscape. Aries' influence can bring a sense of enthusiasm and a willingness to take initiative in various aspects of your life. This lunar transit encourages you to be more decisive and proactive in pursuing your goals and desires. You might notice a boost in confidence and a passion for independence, inspiring you to embrace new challenges with a fearless attitude.

9 Tuesday

The placement of Mars in Libra in the tenth house indicates a strategic and diplomatic approach to career, public image, and authority. Your assertiveness is expressed through a desire for fairness and collaboration in professional endeavors. You may find fulfillment in leadership roles that require tact and negotiation, and your energy is directed toward achieving success through cooperative efforts.

10 Wednesday

Moon ingress Taurus. Taurus' influence brings a sense of calm and contentment, encouraging you to find comfort in life's simple pleasures. During this lunar transit, you may feel more attuned to your physical senses, enjoying the taste of good food, the beauty of nature, or the soothing touch of comforting surroundings. This transit is a favorable time to focus on self-care and nurturing yourself, as the Taurus Moon fosters a sense of security and well-being.

11 Thursday

With the Sun illuminating your expansive ninth house, your Virgo energy is channeled into a quest for knowledge, practical wisdom, and self-improvement. You approach life with a meticulous and analytical mind, seeking to understand the world through practical experience and continuous learning. Your natural curiosity leads you to explore different philosophies, and you find fulfillment in applying your analytical skills to broaden your understanding of the world.

12 Friday

With the Sun forming a sextile aspect to Jupiter, you might feel a surge of optimism and confidence, providing an excellent opportunity for growth and expansion in various areas of your life. This cosmic alignment encourages you to seize opportunities and take a positive outlook on your endeavors. As the Moon moves into Gemini, your emotions may become more adaptable and curious, prompting you to seek new experiences and engage in stimulating conversations.

13 Saturday

The Sun is conjunct with Mercury; you may experience a powerful alignment between your thoughts and self-expression. Your mind is clear, and your communication becomes more articulate and persuasive. During this conjunction, you can convey your ideas with confidence and conviction, making it an excellent time for negotiations, presentations, or any form of public speaking. Your mental agility and quick thinking can lead to problem-solving and decision-making.

14 Sunday

Step into the rhythm of the cosmic dance that influences your daily routine. It is a time to sync with the celestial cadence, infusing your daily activities with a sense of purpose and intentionality. Consider adopting new habits that align with your goals and aspirations. Whether it's incorporating mindfulness practices, setting realistic goals, or prioritizing self-care, allow the cosmic energies to guide you towards a more balanced and fulfilling daily life.

15 Monday

Moon ingress Cancer is an excellent time to spend quality time with loved ones and engage in activities that evoke a sense of nostalgia and familiarity. You may find yourself more empathetic and compassionate, making understanding and supporting those around you easier. Embrace the nurturing energy of the Cancer Moon to cultivate emotional well-being and strengthen your bonds with family and close friends, fostering a sense of emotional fulfillment and contentment.

16 Tuesday

With Venus forming a harmonious sextile with Mars, you may experience enhanced passion and harmony in your relationships. This astrological alignment brings a beautiful balance between your desires and your ability to assert yourself. You feel more confident and magnetic, attracting positive attention and affection. It is an ideal time to express your feelings and desires, as your communication will offer warmth and receptivity.

17 Wednesday

As the Moon moves into Leo, you may feel a surge of confidence and a desire to express yourself more openly. This lunar transit brings a sense of enthusiasm and a need for recognition, inspiring you to shine. However, with Mercury opposing Saturn, you might encounter some mental challenges and communication barriers. Being patient with yourself and others during this time is essential, as you may experience self-doubt or encounter resistance in your conversations.

18 Thursday

As Mercury moves into Libra, you may find yourself more inclined to seek harmony and balance in your communication style. This astrological influence encourages you to weigh both sides of an issue and consider different points of view before forming opinions. However, with Mercury opposed to Neptune, you might experience difficulty maintaining clarity and focus. This aspect can lead to daydreams or getting lost in vague ideas, making it crucial to stay grounded.

19 Friday

As Mercury forms a trine to Uranus and Pluto, you may experience transformative thinking. This astrological alignment fosters an open-minded and innovative approach to problem-solving. Your thoughts may be more profound and insightful, and you could crave topics that stimulate your curiosity. With the Moon's ingress into Virgo and Venus also moving into Virgo, there's an emphasis on practicality and detail in your emotional and relational experiences.

20 Saturday

When Venus forms a square aspect of Uranus, you may experience a period of unpredictability and excitement in your relationships and personal values. This astrological influence can bring sudden changes or disruptions in love, romance, and finances. You might be seeking freedom and novelty in your connections. While this square can be thrilling, it can lead to impulsive decisions and a desire for instant gratification.

21 Sunday

Sun opposed Saturn. New Moon. Moon ingress Libra. Embrace the energy of the New Moon to set intentions for personal growth and find constructive ways to navigate the challenges presented by the Sun-Saturn opposition. Use the harmonious Libra influence to foster understanding and compromise in your external connections and within yourself. It is a time for self-reflection and finding innovative solutions to achieve harmony and success.

22 Monday

As Mars moves into Scorpio, you may experience a shift towards deeper emotions and intense determination. This astrological transit can bring a surge of passion and the desire to explore your desires and motivations. Additionally, with the September Equinox marking a season change, you might need to reassess your priorities. The Sun's ingress into Libra further amplifies this focus on equilibrium and harmony, urging you to seek fairness and cooperation in your interactions.

23 Tuesday

Sun opposed Neptune's astrological aspect, which can cloud your judgment and make it challenging to see things as they are. You might feel more vulnerable and impressionable, making it essential to be cautious of deception or self-deception. This opposition may also bring a sense of disillusionment or a desire to escape from reality. Staying grounded and avoiding making major decisions during this time is essential, as your perceptions may skew.

24 Wednesday

With the Sun forming trines to Uranus and Pluto, you may experience transformative energy and breakthroughs. This astrological alignment enhances your sense of individuality and confidence to embrace change. You might feel drawn to innovative ideas and be more open to taking risks and exploring new possibilities. As the Moon moves into Scorpio, your emotions deepen, and you may seek profound connections and a greater understanding of your inner world.

25 Thursday

Navigate the professional cosmos with a spirit of innovation and adaptability. The celestial energies cast a spotlight on your career path, urging you to embrace new challenges and explore unconventional avenues. This period encourages you to think outside the traditional boundaries, fostering a mindset of creativity and resilience in the professional arena. Trust in the cosmic support as you navigate the currents of your work life, seeking opportunities for growth and advancement.

26 Friday

As the Moon moves into Sagittarius, you may experience a shift in your emotional energy, embracing a sense of optimism and adventure. Sagittarius' influence encourages you to expand your horizons and seek new experiences that nurture your sense of freedom and exploration. During this lunar transition, you might be more open to learning, seeking knowledge, and engaging in philosophical discussions.

27 Saturday

Within the cosmic atelier of creativity, let the radiant hues of inspiration paint your world. Embrace the freedom to explore your artistic self, whether through visual arts, writing, or other creative expressions. Like a cosmic muse, let the celestial energies inspire innovation and encourage the breaking of creative boundaries. This period invites you to dance with the vibrant palette of creativity, allowing your artistic endeavors to be a celestial celebration of self-expression.

28 Sunday

As the cosmic gardener tends to the landscape of your daily life, feel the gentle breeze of change rustling through your routines. Embrace the opportunity to nurture new habits and rituals that align with your goals. Just as the cosmic currents effortlessly sway through the branches, let your daily activities flow with purpose and mindfulness. This period encourages you to plant seeds of intentionality, cultivating a rhythm that blossoms into a garden of fulfillment.

OCTOBER

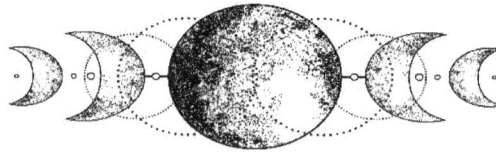

MOON MAGIC

Sun	Mon	Tue	Wed	Thu	Fri	Sat
			1	2	3	4
5	6	7	8	9	10	11
12	13	14	15	16	17	18
19	20	21	22	23	24	25
26	27	28	29	30	31	

New Moon

HUNTERS MOON

29 Monday

Moon ingress Capricorn astrological influence encourages you to be practical and disciplined in your approach to your feelings and goals. The Capricorn Moon fosters a sense of responsibility and a desire for achievement, making it an excellent time to set clear intentions and work diligently towards them. This lunar transit also enhances your ability to stay composed under pressure and navigate challenges with determination and resilience.

30 Tuesday

The Sun in Libra graces your tenth house, enhancing your career and public image with a diplomatic and refined aura. You are driven to achieve success through cooperation and collaboration, often finding fulfillment in roles that allow you to bring people together. Strive to balance your desire for harmony with the need for decisive leadership, as your ability to navigate conflicts gracefully can be an influential asset in your professional life.

1 Wednesday

As the Moon moves into Aquarius, you may experience a shift towards a more open and forward-thinking emotional state. This astrological influence encourages you to embrace individuality and connect with like-minded people. Your emotions may become more detached and rational, allowing you to view situations from a broader perspective. However, with Mercury square Jupiter, there may be a tendency to exaggerate or overlook details in communication.

2 Thursday

With Mars in Scorpio in the eleventh house, your approach to friendships, group activities, and societal pursuits is marked by passion, depth, and a desire for meaningful connections. You assert yourself assertively within social circles, often taking a leadership role or contributing to collective goals with intensity. Your energy is directed toward causes that align with your deeply held values, and you draw friendships that involve mutual support and transformative growth.

3 Friday

With Venus in Virgo influencing your approach to travel, higher education, and philosophical pursuits, your love for order and practicality extends to your expansive worldview. You find pleasure in exploring intellectual and philosophical concepts that have real-world applications. Your energy is directed toward transformative experiences through learning and expanding your beliefs in a practical and structured manner.

4 Saturday

Moon ingress Pisces astrological influence encourages you to connect with your inner world, allowing your feelings to flow freely. Pisces' energy fosters compassion and empathy, making it an excellent time to nurture your relationships and support those in need. You might draw artistic and creative pursuits and seek moments of solace and reflection. Let the soulful energy of the Pisces Moon nurture your emotional well-being and offer emotional healing.

5 Sunday

Embark on a cosmic journey into the realms of self-discovery as planetary energies align to illuminate your inner landscape. This introspective phase encourages you to delve into the depths of your thoughts. Embrace moments of solitude and contemplation, allowing the celestial forces to guide you on a profound quest for self-understanding. In this introspective odyssey, you may uncover hidden facets of your personality, paving the way for a renewed sense of purpose.

6 Monday

Moon ingress Aries. Mercury ingress Scorpio. You may draw investigative or research-oriented activities that challenge your analytical skills. Embrace the Aries Moon's dynamic energy to ignite your passions and embrace the Mercury in Scorpio influence to engage in introspection and delve into the depths of your mind, fostering a balanced and transformative approach to your emotions and intellectual pursuits.

7 Tuesday

During a Full Moon, you may experience heightened emotions and a sense of culmination in various aspects of your life. This astrological phase marks a time of revelation and clarity, revealing what has been hidden or brewing beneath the surface. However, with Mercury square Pluto, there could be a tendency for intense communication. This aspect might lead to power struggles in discussions or a need to dig deeper into matters, potentially uncovering hidden motives.

8 Wednesday

Moon ingress Taurus astrological shift encourages you to seek pleasure and contentment in life's simple and sensual aspects. Taurus' energy fosters an appreciation for beauty and the finer things, making it a favorable time to indulge in sensory delights and enjoy the present moment. Simultaneously, with Venus sextile Jupiter, you'll likely feel a boost in positivity and an inclination towards optimism in your relationships and creative endeavors.

9 Thursday

Propel yourself into an inspiring journey of self-improvement, where the emphasis on enhancing your situation becomes the guiding star. As you navigate this cosmic path, rising prospects unveil themselves, revealing the secrets to expanding your life outwardly. Discover a novel approach that injects momentum into your world, and with the acceleration of life's pace, find yourself uplifted by the promising results of your efforts.

10 Friday

Moon ingress Gemini's astrological influence encourages you to engage your mind and seek intellectual stimulation. Gemini's energy fosters a desire for variety and a willingness to explore different ideas and perspectives. You might seek conversations, social interactions, and learning opportunities during this lunar transition. Your emotions become more adaptable and light-hearted, allowing you to connect with others engagingly.

11 Saturday

When Venus opposes Saturn, you may encounter emotional challenges and limitations in your relationships. This astrological aspect can bring feelings of distance or even a sense of loneliness. You might experience restrictions or delays in matters of the heart, leading to a need for patience and introspection. This opposition encourages you to assess the practical aspects of your relationships, ensuring that they are built on a solid foundation and aligned with your goals.

12 Sunday

Moon ingress Cancer's astrological influence encourages you to connect with your feelings deeper and seek comfort and security. Cancer's energy fosters a sense of empathy and a desire to care for yourself and others. You might find solace in spending time with loved ones or creating a cozy and harmonious environment at home. This lunar transit enhances your intuition and sensitivity, making it an ideal time to tune into your emotions and reflect on your needs.

13 Monday

Venus ingress Libra's energy fosters a desire for fairness and social grace, making it an excellent time to engage in diplomacy and compromise. You might crave to be around art, culture, and activities that bring aesthetic pleasure during this transit. Embrace the Venus in Libra energy to enhance social interactions, foster meaningful connections, and create an atmosphere of peace and equilibrium in your personal and professional life.

14 Tuesday

The Venus trine Uranus and Venus trine Pluto aspects add an intriguing layer of intensity and excitement to your relationships and personal growth. These harmonious alignments offer opportunities for new connections and the potential for profound emotional transformation. Embrace this dynamic interplay of energies to navigate romantic idealism, harness the power of Pluto's transformative influence, and infuse connections with passion and authenticity.

15 Wednesday

Follow the cosmic compass as it points towards the pathways of exploration and expansion in your intellectual pursuits. The stars encourage you to embark on a journey of learning and discovery, whether through formal education, self-study, or engaging conversations. Like a cosmic scholar, let the celestial energies broaden your horizons, guiding you toward the wisdom that resides in the expansive universe of knowledge.

16 Thursday

With the Moon moving into Virgo, you might notice a shift towards a more practical and detail-oriented approach to your emotions. This astrological influence encourages you to pay attention to the finer points of daily life. Virgo's energy fosters a sense of organization and a desire for efficiency, making it an excellent time to tackle tasks. During this lunar transit, you may find satisfaction in caring for practical matters and improving order and structure.

17 Friday

When the Sun forms a square aspect to Jupiter, you may experience a period of enthusiasm and optimism, but it's crucial to avoid overextending yourself. This astrological influence can bring a tendency to take on too much or to be overly confident in your endeavors. While the combination of the Sun and Jupiter can enhance your sense of self-belief and ambition, it's essential to maintain a realistic perspective and consider the potential consequences of your actions.

18 Saturday

Immerse yourself in the cosmic seas of emotional intelligence, where the stars encourage you to explore the depths of your feelings and connections with others. This period invites you to navigate the emotional constellations, fostering a greater understanding of your own emotions and those of the cosmic beings around you. Trust in the celestial currents to guide you toward a period of enhanced emotional awareness and harmonious connections.

19 Sunday

Moon ingress Libra astrological transition encourages you to seek balance and cooperation in your interactions with others. Libra's energy fosters a desire for fairness and diplomacy, making it a favorable time to engage in meaningful conversations and connect with those around you. During this lunar transit, you might find yourself more attuned to the needs and feelings of others, valuing their perspectives and seeking to find common ground.

20 Monday

Mercury conjunct Mars astrological alignment amplifies your communication style and intellectual drive, encouraging you to express your thoughts and ideas more assertively. Your mind becomes sharper and more focused, enabling you to tackle challenges head-on and confidently make decisions. This conjunction can also spark mental energy, inspiring you to take on new tasks and enthusiastically engage in debates or discussions.

21 Tuesday

New Moon. Moon ingress Scorpio. It is a time for self-discovery and embracing transformational changes. As you align your intentions with the New Moon's energy, use the Scorpio influence to release what no longer serves you and embark on a journey of personal growth and empowerment. Embrace the profound insights that this combination of the New Moon and Scorpio offers to foster a period of renewal and meaningful transformation in various aspects of your life.

22 Wednesday

With Neptune moving into Pisces, you may experience a heightened imagination and intuition. This astrological transition encourages you to connect with your spiritual side and explore the realm of dreams and creativity. Neptune's energy fosters a sense of empathy and compassion, urging you to be more attuned to the emotions of others. During this cosmic shift, you might find yourself drawn to artistic and mystical pursuits, seeking inspiration from the intangible and ethereal.

23 Thursday

Sun ingress Scorpio's astrological transition encourages you to embrace life's mysteries and delve into your psyche's hidden aspects. Scorpio's energy fosters a desire for transformation and rebirth, urging you to let go of what no longer serves you and welcome new beginnings. During this solar transit, you might find yourself drawn to matters of depth and intensity, seeking to uncover truths and understand the underlying motivations behind actions and emotions.

24 Friday

With the Moon moving into Sagittarius, you might experience a sense of adventure and a desire for exploration. This astrological influence encourages you to seek new experiences and broaden your horizons. However, the Sun square Pluto can bring about intense transformation and potential power struggles. It's crucial to approach challenges with resilience and integrity, avoiding manipulation or control tactics.

25 Saturday

When Mercury forms a trine aspect to Saturn, you may experience increased mental discipline and focused communication. This astrological alignment enhances your ability to think and speak precisely and practically. Your thoughts become organized, and you may find it easier to plan and execute tasks efficiently. This trine encourages a balanced approach to problem-solving, allowing you to combine your analytical skills with a patient and methodical mindset.

26 Sunday

As the Moon moves into Capricorn, you may notice a more focused and disciplined emotional state. This astrological influence encourages you to approach your feelings with a practical and responsible mindset. Capricorn's energy fosters a desire for structure, making it an excellent time to set goals and work diligently toward them. You might find satisfaction in aligning your emotions with your long-term aspirations during this lunar transition.

27 Monday

A vital shift forward brings expansion. It does link you up with a new chapter that enables you to circulate in your broader community. Necessary changes occur that attract the right people into your life. It does bring a social time that allows you to gain traction on your vision. It paves the way forward toward a lively and productive inspirational chapter. It attracts wellness and harmony, re-fueling your inspiration and drawing laughter and kinship.

28 Tuesday

With Mars forming a trine to Jupiter, you may experience increased energy and optimism. This astrological alignment enhances your drive and enthusiasm, encouraging you to take bold actions and confidently pursue your goals. Your efforts are likely to be met with success, as this trine brings a sense of expansion and abundance. You might find yourself more willing to take risks and explore new opportunities, supported by a strong belief in your abilities.

29 Wednesday

Moon ingress Aquarius astrological shift encourages you to embrace your unique ideas and connect with a broader community. With Mercury forming a trine to Neptune, your thoughts and communication gain inspiration and imagination, fostering creative and empathetic interactions. As Mercury moves into Sagittarius, your thinking becomes more expansive and open-minded, encouraging you to seek new perspectives and engage in philosophical discussions.

30 Thursday

With Mercury forming a sextile to Pluto, you may experience a period of heightened mental intensity and depth. This astrological alignment enhances your ability to delve into profound subjects and uncover hidden truths. Your thoughts become more perceptive and analytical, allowing you to penetrate beneath the surface of matters. This sextile encourages transformative insights and meaningful conversations that have a lasting impact.

NOVEMBER

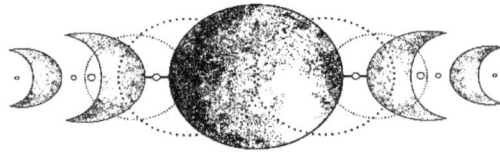

MOON MAGIC

Sun	Mon	Tue	Wed	Thu	Fri	Sat
						1
2	3	4	5	6	7	8
9	10	11	12	13	14	15
16	17	18	19	20	21	22
23	24	25	26	27	28	29
30						

New Moon

BEAVER MOON

31 Friday

Moon ingress Pisces astrological transition encourages you to connect with your inner world and embrace your emotions with compassion and empathy. Pisces' energy fosters a sense of imagination and sensitivity, making it an ideal time to engage in creative pursuits or immerse yourself in the arts. During this lunar transit, you might find solace in moments of solitude and reflection, allowing your feelings to flow freely and uncovering profound layers of the emotional landscape.

1 Saturday

In the visionary eleventh house, your Scorpio Sun aligns with a desire for transformative and authentic connections within your social circles. Your intense and passionate nature makes you a powerful force for change within groups, and you may be drawn to causes or movements that aim to bring about profound transformation. Be aware of the potential for power struggles within friendships and groups, and use your influence to foster positive change and empowerment.

2 Sunday

With the Moon moving into Aries, you may experience dynamic energy and assertiveness. This astrological shift encourages you to take the lead and assert your desires. Aries' energy fosters a sense of independence and a willingness to initiate action. However, with Venus square Jupiter, there's potential for excessive indulgence or unrealistic expectations in matters of the heart. This aspect can bring a tendency to overreach in seeking pleasure or connection.

3 Monday

You dive into the cosmic ocean of improving circumstances, where the emphasis on bettering your situation initiates a journey teeming with inspiration. Rising prospects emerge like celestial waves, unraveling the code that expands the celestial landscape of your life. Embrace a fresh approach that surges momentum, quickening the cosmic tempo and leaving you buoyed by the positive results blossoming from your proactive efforts.

4 Tuesday

The Mars opposition to Uranus can introduce an element of unpredictability and potential disruptions in your plans. While the Mars-Neptune trine enhances your ability to navigate challenges gracefully, the Mars-Uranus opposition encourages you to be adaptable and open to changes. Embrace the combined energy of these aspects to expand your horizons, seek comfort in life's simple pleasures, and approach any unforeseen events with a spirit of flexibility and resilience.

5 Wednesday

The Full Moon astrological phase marks a time of illumination, where the light of the Sun fully reflects upon the Moon, casting a spotlight on your emotions and intentions. It's a moment to reflect on what has come to fruition since the previous New Moon and to release what no longer serves you. The Full Moon encourages you to balance your inner world and your external experiences, providing an opportunity for self-awareness and growth.

6 Thursday

Mars sextile Pluto astrological alignment empowers you to initiate transformative changes in your life. As the Moon moves into Gemini, your emotions become more adaptable and communicative. You might find yourself engaging in lively conversations and seeking out mental stimulation. Simultaneously, Venus moving into Scorpio adds a touch of intensity to your relationships and desires. It is a time for delving into the emotional nuances of connections and embracing authenticity.

7 Friday

As Mars moves through your 12th house, your inner world and subconscious realms become energized with assertive and transformative forces. You may find yourself drawn to solitary pursuits that involve self-reflection, spiritual practices, or uncovering hidden truths. Your subconscious desires are brought to the forefront, and you may experience a surge of energy in navigating the depths of your psyche.

8 Saturday

Uranus ingress Taurus astrological transition can bring innovative and sometimes disruptive energies to financial matters, personal values, and your sense of security. The Venus square Pluto aspect adds intensity to your relationships and desires, potentially leading to power struggles or transformations in heart matters. As the Moon moves into Cancer, your emotions become more attuned to your inner world and connections with loved ones.

9 Sunday

As Mercury turns retrograde, you may encounter a period of introspection and review. This astrological phase encourages you to revisit and reconsider your plans, communications, and decisions. It's a time when misunderstandings and miscommunications can occur more quickly, so practicing patience and clarity in your interactions is advisable. This retrograde invites you to slow down and reflect on matters needing adjustment or refinement.

10 Monday

With the Moon moving into Leo, you may notice a shift toward a more expressive and confident emotional state. This astrological transition encourages you to embrace your creativity and seek opportunities to shine. Leo's energy fosters a desire for recognition and a willingness to share your authentic self with others. During this lunar transit, you might crave activities that allow you to showcase your talents and take center stage.

11 Tuesday

As Jupiter turns retrograde, you may experience a period of introspection and inner growth. This astrological shift encourages you to revisit your beliefs, values, and areas of expansion in your life. While Jupiter's direct motion often brings external opportunities, its retrograde phase encourages you to explore the internal aspects of these opportunities. It's a time to reflect on your goals, aspirations, and how you've been expanding your horizons.

12 Wednesday

With Mercury conjunct Mars, you may experience a period of heightened mental agility and assertiveness. This astrological alignment empowers you to think quickly and communicate your thoughts with directness and determination. Your mind becomes sharper and your words more impactful, making it a suitable time for taking action on your ideas and expressing your opinions. As the Moon moves into Virgo, your emotions may become more analytical and detail-oriented.

13 Thursday

As Venus graces your eleventh house, your social circles and affiliations become arenas of beauty, harmony, and connection. Friendships take on a special significance, and you find joy in collaborative efforts that align with your values. Your ability to foster positive relationships within your networks makes this a period conducive to forming fulfilling friendships. Your love for shared experiences and common goals brings a sense of unity to your social interactions.

14 Friday

With Venus in Scorpio in the eleventh house, your approach to friendships, group activities, and societal pursuits is marked by intensity, emotional depth, and a desire for meaningful connections. You express through transformative and passionate engagement. Your energy is directed toward creating powerful and authentic connections within your social circles, and you may be drawn to friendships that involve mutual support and shared transformative experiences.

15 Saturday

As the Moon moves into Libra, you may notice a shift towards a greater emphasis on balance and harmony in your emotions and interactions. This astrological transition encourages you to seek fairness and cooperation in your relationships. Libra's energy fosters a desire for companionship and a willingness to find common ground. During this lunar transition, you might seek social activities and engage in conversations that create understanding and unity.

16 Sunday

With Mars in Sagittarius influencing your twelfth house, your energy and assertiveness are directed toward the realms of spirituality, hidden knowledge, and the subconscious. You may find fulfillment in solitary pursuits that involve exploration of your inner world or spiritual practices. Your assertiveness may manifest in behind-the-scenes roles, where your passion for seeking higher understanding can contribute to transformative experiences.

17 Monday

As the Moon moves into Scorpio, your emotions may become more probing. This combination encourages you to explore deeper emotional currents. Embrace the Sun trines' energy to blend your aspirations with steady determination, while the Mercury-Pluto sextile enhances your ability to articulate your thoughts with depth and conviction. Allow the Scorpio Moon to guide you in introspection and emotional authenticity as you navigate this dynamic balance.

18 Tuesday

In the vast cosmic tapestry of your career, weave threads of optimism and positivity. The sunlit beams of success illuminate your journey, bringing clarity and warmth to your professional pursuits. Embrace the interconnectedness of your professional endeavors with the celestial currents. This period encourages you to view your career as a part of a larger cosmic design, where each step forward contributes to the harmonious unfolding of your professional destiny.

19 Wednesday

Mercury ingress Scorpio astrological transition encourages you to delve beneath the surface and explore deeper meanings in your interactions. The Mercury-Uranus opposition can bring unexpected shifts and disruptions in your thinking patterns and conversations, urging you to be flexible and open to unconventional ideas. Yet, the Mercury-Neptune trine adds a touch of intuition and creativity to your communication, allowing for more empathetic and imaginative expression.

20 Thursday

During a New Moon, you may experience a sense of fresh beginnings and opportunities for setting intentions. This astrological phase marks a time of planting seeds for the future and embarking on new ventures. With the Sun conjunct Mercury, your thoughts and communication align with your sense of self. As Mercury moves into Sagittarius, your thinking becomes more expansive and open to exploring new horizons.

21 Friday

With the Sun in opposition to Uranus, you may experience a period of unexpected shifts and heightened restlessness. This astrological alignment can bring about a desire for independence and a need for change. You may find routines and plans disrupting, and you could seek more freedom and spontaneity. However, the Sun's trine to Neptune adds a harmonious influence, encouraging you to embrace a more intuitive and compassionate approach.

22 Saturday

With the Sun moving into Sagittarius, you may feel more adventurous and expansive energy. Embrace the Sagittarius Sun's energy to embrace curiosity and open-mindedness while utilizing the Mercury-Saturn trine to organize your thoughts effectively. Let the Capricorn Moon's influence guide you in tackling tasks with determination, and allow the Mercury-Jupiter trine to inspire your exploration of new ideas and perspectives during this dynamic period of growth.

23 Sunday

With the Sun forming a sextile to Pluto, you may experience empowering transformation and increased insight. This astrological alignment empowers you to delve into deeper layers of your identity and profoundly embrace change. This sextile encourages you to tap into your inner strength and resources to shift your life positively. You might find yourself drawn to uncovering hidden truths and exploring the motivations behind your actions.

24 Monday

Infuse your social and creative endeavors with the cosmic glow of optimistic intentions. Envision a future where your interactions are marked by positivity, creativity, and shared inspiration. Allow the celestial forces to guide you toward promoting your social and creative pursuits to encourage them to flourish in a harmonious dance of cosmic energy. Your social connections deepen as the cosmic energies guide you toward fostering a community of support and joy.

25 Tuesday

Mercury conjunct Venus. Moon ingress Aquarius. This combination encourages you to engage in conversations that stimulate your intellect and connect with like-minded individuals who share your innovative ideas. Embrace the Mercury-Venus conjunction's energy to express your feelings eloquently while using the Aquarius Moon's influence to foster collaboration and embrace your unique perspectives.

26 Wednesday

With Venus forming trines to Jupiter and Saturn, you may experience a balanced and harmonious energy in relationships and values. This astrological alignment gives you a sense of abundance and stability in your connections and desires. The Venus trine Jupiter aspect encourages positive growth and expansion in your interactions, while the Venus trine Saturn aspect brings a grounded and disciplined approach to matters of the heart.

27 Thursday

On Thanksgiving, as the Moon moves into Pisces, you may find a sense of emotional depth and a desire for compassion and connection with loved ones. This astrological transition encourages you to embrace a spirit of empathy and togetherness during this memorable holiday. Pisces' energy fosters a sense of unity and a willingness to express gratitude for the blessings in your life. It's a time to reflect on what you're thankful for and to share your appreciation.

28 Friday

As Saturn turns direct, you may experience a shift in the cosmic energies that influence your sense of responsibility and discipline. This astrological phenomenon marks a time when Saturn, the taskmaster of the zodiac, begins to move forward again after a period of retrograde motion. With this change, it brings a renewed sense of structure and determination. It's an opportune moment to revisit and recommit to your long-term goals and responsibilities.

29 Saturday

As Mercury turns direct, you may notice a shift in the flow of communication and decision-making. This astrological event marks the end of potential miscommunications, technical glitches, and delays often accompanying Mercury retrograde. With Mercury moving forward, you'll likely experience increased clarity and a sense of progress in various aspects of your life. It's an excellent time to implement any insights or revisions you made during the retrograde phase.

30 Sunday

As Venus enters Sagittarius, your approach to love and beauty becomes more adventurous and open-minded. Embrace the Aries Moon's energy to assert your needs and desires while using the Venus-Neptune trine to foster emotional connection and creative expression. Allow Venus in Sagittarius to inspire you to explore new horizons in your relationships and aesthetic preferences as you navigate this period with a blend of independence and compassion.

DECEMBER

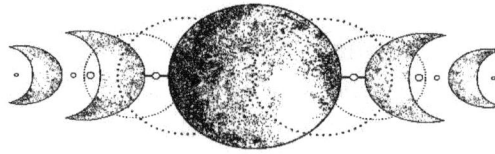

MOON MAGIC

Sun	Mon	Tue	Wed	Thu	Fri	Sat
	1	2	3	4	5	6
7	8	9	10	11	12	13
14	15	16	17	18	19	20
21	22	23	24	25	26	27
28	29	30	31			

New Moon

COLD MOON

DECEMBER

1 Monday

Let the vibrant hues of optimism paint the canvas of your career as you embark on this growth-driven phase. Feel the cosmic brushstrokes creating a masterpiece of success and fulfillment. Embrace the positive energy that surrounds you, infusing every aspect of your professional life with the celestial glow of hope and possibility. This month is a time to radiate optimism and attract the abundance that the cosmic forces have in store for your career journey.

2 Tuesday

As the Moon moves into Taurus, you might notice a shift towards a more grounded and practical emotional state. This astrological transition encourages you to seek comfort and stability in your surroundings and relationships. With Venus forming a sextile to Pluto, your interactions and connections may take on a deeper, more profound quality. This aspect can foster a sense of emotional intensity and transformation in your personal and romantic relationships.

3 Wednesday

With Mercury in Scorpio in the eleventh house, your communication and thought processes are directed toward friendships, group activities, and societal pursuits with intensity, depth, and a desire for meaningful connections. You express your ideas assertively within social circles, often contributing to group discussions with a focus on transformative and profound insights. Your energy is directed toward creating powerful and authentic connections within your social networks.

4 Thursday

With the Moon moving into Gemini, you may experience a shift towards a more curious and communicative emotional state. This astrological transition encourages you to engage in lively conversations, seek out information, and connect with others intellectually. However, emotions could be running high and culminating as it's also a Full Moon. Full Moons are a time of illumination and realization, often bringing underlying issues to the surface.

5 Friday

Cast your social net wide as the cosmic currents beckon you to set intentions for expansive connections and shared experiences. As your social sphere blossoms, your relationships deepen in authenticity and mutual understanding. It is a time to lay the groundwork for a vibrant and harmonious social tapestry guided by the celestial forces that encourage positive connections and communal growth. You cultivate friendships that resonate with positivity and connection.

6 Saturday

With the Moon moving into Cancer, you may become more emotionally sensitive and nurturing. This astrological transition encourages you to seek comfort and security in your surroundings and with your loved ones. Cancer's energy fosters a connection to your emotions and a desire to care for others. Additionally, Mercury's formation of a trine with Neptune makes your communication and thoughts more intuitive and imaginative.

7 Sunday

The cosmic winds of positive change gently sweep through your domestic sphere. Embrace the opportunity to declutter both physical and emotional spaces, creating room for fresh energy and revitalization. Whether through rearranging furniture, fostering open communication with family members, or exploring new ways to infuse warmth into your living environment, let the celestial currents guide you in cultivating a harmonious and supportive home base.

8 Monday

Illuminate your daily work routine with the radiant energy of the cosmos. The stars invite you to infuse each moment with positivity and optimism, creating a celestial rhythm that resonates with joy. You find inspiration in the small details of your work, allowing the cosmic currents to lift your spirits and make the day a celestial celebration of your professional journey. The stars encourage a harmonious environment, fostering camaraderie among your colleagues.

9 Tuesday

Mars square Saturn's astrological aspect can bring about a sense of frustration and a need for patience in pursuing your goals. It's important to know that progress might be slower during this time, and your challenges could test your determination. However, the Mars-Saturn square also offers an opportunity to develop a stronger work ethic and a more disciplined approach to achieving your objectives.

10 Wednesday

With the Moon moving into Virgo, you may notice a more analytical and detail-oriented emotional state. This astrological transition encourages you to focus on practical matters and strive for order and efficiency in your daily life. Virgo's energy fosters a desire for organization and a meticulous approach to problem-solving. Additionally, with Neptune turning direct, you may experience a newfound clarity and inspiration in your dreams and intuitive insights.

11 Thursday

As Mercury moves into Sagittarius, your thinking becomes more expansive and open to new ideas and perspectives. This transition encourages you to explore the broader horizons of knowledge and engage in philosophical discussions. Embrace the Mercury-Neptune trine's energy to express your ideas with sensitivity and depth while allowing the Mercury in Sagittarius influence to inspire your intellectual curiosity and encourage you to seek new experiences and insights.

12 Friday

Moon ingress Libra celestial transition encourages you to appreciate beauty, seek balance, and nurture connections with others. Libra's energy fosters a deep appreciation for aesthetics and a strong desire to create a peaceful and fair environment. During this lunar influence, you could find yourself drawn to social gatherings and engaging in conversations that foster understanding and cooperation.

13 Saturday

Mercury sextile Pluto astrological alignment empowers you to delve deep into matters and seek hidden truths. Your mind becomes a tool for transformation, enabling you to uncover hidden layers of understanding and make significant discoveries. Engage in research, explore complex subjects, or have conversations that go beneath the surface today. Mercury-Pluto sextile's energy empowers your communication and thinking, allowing you to navigate situations precisely.

14 Sunday

Mars square Neptune. Be cautious of potential misunderstandings or misplaced energy. While this aspect can pose challenges, it can remind you to tap into your intuition and use your actions and desires to align with your higher ideals and dreams. Embrace the Mars-Neptune square as an opportunity to explore a more imaginative and intuitive approach to your goals. Still, remain grounded and transparent in your intentions to avoid potential pitfalls.

15 Monday

With the Moon moving into Scorpio and Mars entering Capricorn, you may sense a shift in the emotional and energetic atmosphere. This astrological transition can deepen emotions and a more focused, determined approach to your actions. The Scorpio Moon encourages introspection, intensity, and a desire to explore hidden facets of your inner world. It's a time when emotions may run deep, and you might find yourself drawn to matters that require unwavering commitment.

16 Tuesday

The lush garden of your professional endeavors blossoms with vibrant possibilities. A role you actively participate in developing takes flight, soaring towards rising prospects. The cosmic energy infuses this endeavor with the essence of success. Trust in the expansive energy of the universe as it guides you towards a bright horizon. As the seeds of your efforts sprout, witness the celestial magic unfold, bringing forth a bountiful harvest of achievements and accolades.

17 Wednesday

Sun square Saturn's astrological aspect can clash with your desire for self-expression and responsibility demands. You may need to confront limitations or face challenges that test your patience and perseverance. However, as the Moon moves into Sagittarius, you'll find a spark of optimism and a desire for adventure. This lunar transition encourages you to seek new horizons and explore growth opportunities, even in adversity.

18 Thursday

As the cosmic energies weave through the fabric of your career, a clear goal comes into focus like a guiding star in the night sky. The celestial forces encourage you to dream big, setting your sights on ambitious aspirations. With a strategic plan as your cosmic map, chart the stepping stones that lead toward the realization of your goals. Trust in the celestial guidance as you navigate the cosmic journey towards success.

19 Friday

Expand your horizons in the cosmic tapestry of networking and social connections. The stars align to bring positive and uplifting individuals into your professional sphere. Embrace the celestial energy that fosters meaningful connections, creating a supportive network that propels you towards collective success. Trust in the cosmic currents to guide you in cultivating relationships that contribute to your overall fulfillment and happiness.

20 Saturday

The New Moon astrological phase marks a time of renewal and planting the seeds of your desires. As the Moon moves into Capricorn, you may find a heightened sense of discipline and responsibility, aligning well with the New Moon's energy for setting practical goals and working steadily toward them. Additionally, the Black Moon's shift into Sagittarius brings a sense of expansion and exploration to your inner world by delving into the deeper aspects of your beliefs and intentions.

21 Sunday

The December Solstice marks a turning point in the year, symbolizing a shift towards longer days and the promise of renewed energy. As the Sun moves into Capricorn, you're encouraged to embrace a goal-oriented approach to your ambitions. Use this cosmic interplay as an opportunity to pause and reflect, ensuring your intentions are clear and align with your long-term goals. Despite the potential challenges, this period offers a good chance for inner growth.

22 Monday

Moon ingress Aquarius. You might be drawn to unique ideas, progressive causes, and group activities promoting community and belonging during this lunar transit. Use the Aquarius Moon's energy to engage in discussions that challenge your perspective and connect with others. It's a time to explore your intellectual pursuits, celebrate diversity, and embrace your role within the collective as you navigate this period with an open heart and a curious mind.

23 Tuesday

Enjoy the celestial influence of your home life, bringing the positive energy of your career growth into your sanctuary. Create a cosmic balance between your professional ambitions and the comforts of home. This period invites you to celebrate achievements with loved ones, turning your home into a celestial haven where success is not only acknowledged but embraced with warmth and joy. It is a time of blessings and celebration in a season of giving and sharing.

24 Wednesday

With Venus forming a square to Neptune, you may navigate a period of romantic or idealistic confusion. This astrological aspect can create an illusion or ambiguity in the heart and aesthetics. It's essential to exercise caution in relationships and financial matters during this time, as things may not be as they initially appear. Simultaneously, as Venus moves into Capricorn, more practical energy enters your love life and personal values.

25 Thursday

Moon ingress Pisces astrological transition encourages you to embrace the spirit of empathy, making it an excellent time to connect with loved ones and spread warmth and goodwill. Pisces' energy fosters a dreamy and artistic atmosphere, inviting you to engage in creative and imaginative activities. It's a day for reflection, gratitude, and sharing love with those who matter most. You may find solace in acts of kindness, art, or simply spending time in quiet contemplation.

26 Friday

With the Sun in Capricorn influencing your first house, your personality is characterized by ambition, determination, and a focus on achieving long-term goals. You project a sense of authority and responsibility, and a desire marks your self-expression for success and recognition. Your approach to life is disciplined and organized, and you may find fulfillment in leadership roles that allow you to showcase your competence and expertise.

27 Saturday

Moon ingress Aries astrological transition encourages you to embrace a more assertive and action-oriented approach to endeavors. Aries' energy fosters a desire for independence and self-expression, prompting you to take the lead and enthusiastically pursue your goals. During this lunar transit, you might feel a boost in confidence and a willingness to tackle challenges head-on. It's an ideal time to initiate projects, set goals, and channel your emotions into productive activities.

28 Sunday

With Mercury in Sagittarius influencing your twelfth house, your thoughts and communication style are directed toward the realms of spirituality, hidden knowledge, and the subconscious. You may find fulfillment in solitary pursuits involving higher learning, philosophical reflection, or spiritual practices. Your communication may be visionary and insightful, often expressing a desire for profound understanding.

29 Monday

Moon ingress Taurus astrological transition encourages you to seek comfort, security, and a deeper connection to the physical world. Taurus' energy fosters a desire for simplicity and a slower, deliberate pace. You may find yourself drawn to activities that soothe your senses and engage your appreciation for life's pleasures, whether enjoying a delicious meal or spending time in nature. This lunar influence invites you to step back and savor the simple joys of existence.

30 Tuesday

When Mercury forms a square aspect with Saturn, challenges related to communication and mental processes may arise. You might find that your thoughts and ideas encounter obstacles or resistance, making it harder to express yourself effectively. It can feel like there's a constant tension between your desire to communicate and Saturn's restrictive influence, which can manifest as self-doubt or a tendency to be overly critical of your thoughts and words.

31 Wednesday

As the Moon moves into Gemini on New Year's Eve, you may experience a shift in your emotional energy and social interactions. This lunar ingress can bring a sense of curiosity and restlessness to your celebrations, making you more inclined to engage in lively conversations and seek out new experiences. You might find yourself drawn to variety and diversity, enjoying the company of different people and exploring a range of interests throughout the evening.

1 Thursday

On New Year's Day, as Mercury ingresses into Capricorn while simultaneously forming a square aspect with Neptune, you may encounter a mix of practicality and confusion in your thinking and communication. You might desire to set clear, ambitious goals for the year ahead, aligning with Capricorn's goal-oriented energy. However, the challenging square with Neptune could introduce a degree of ambiguity, making it essential to stay grounded in your approach.

Astrology, Tarot & Horoscope Books.

Mystic Cat

www.ingramcontent.com/pod-product-compliance
Lightning Source LLC
Chambersburg PA
CBHW080531090426

42733CB00015B/2548